THE MISANTHROPE

Molière
a new version by
Constance Congdon

from a literal translation by
Virginia Scott

BROADWAY PLAY PUBLISHING INC
56 E 81st St., NY NY 10028-0202
212 772-8334 fax: 212 772-8358
http://www.BroadwayPlayPubl.com

THE MISANTHROPE
© Copyright 2003 by Constance Congdon

First printing: September 2003
I S B N: 0-88145-205-X

Book design: Marie Donovan
Word processing: Microsoft Word for Windows
Typographic controls: Xerox Ventura Publisher 2.0 P E
Typeface: Palatino
Copy editing: Sue Gilad
Printed on recycled acid-free paper and bound in the
U S A

CONTENTS

ABOUT THE AUTHOR

Constance Congdon's most well-known play, TALES OF THE LOST FORMICANS, has been produced in Helsinki, Brixton, Manchester, Tokyo and over 100 productions all over the United States, in New York City by the Women's Project and then in a very successful revival by the Monster[less] Theatre in 1996. Her plays CASANOVA and DOG OPERA were both produced at the Joseph Papp Public Theatre in New York. She also has written librettos for four operas and eight plays for children, one of which went to the Moscow Central Children's Theatre in 1989. Her play about the first woman president, LIPS, was commissioned by Spielberg's Dreamworks through Playwrights Horizons and was produced at Primary Stages in New York in 1998. The Profile Theater in Portland, Oregon devoted an entire season to her works and their production of NO MERCY included a new companion piece that is called ONE DAY EARLIER. THE AUTOMATIC PIETÀ and MOONTEL SIX are plays she wrote for the American Conservatory Theater in San Francisco's Young Conservatory. MOONTEL SIX received several productions in the U K and Northern Ireland, one of which went to the Connections Festival at the Royal National Theatre in July 2003.

Congdon's play DOG OPERA is published by Samuel French and also is included in *The Actor's Book of Gay and Lesbian Plays*. A book of four of her plays, *Tales of the Lost Formicans and Other Plays*, is published by Theater

Communications Group. Broadway Plays publishes the actor's editions of TALES OF THE LOST FORMICANS, LIPS, and A SERVANT OF TWO MASTERS.

Congdon's play MOTHER, based on Gorky's play VASSA ZHELEZNOVA, starring Olympia Dukakis, will be produced at the American Conservatory Theater in the spring of 2004.

Congdon is an alumna of New Dramatists, a member of PEN and currently teaches playwriting at Amherst College and the Yale School of Drama.

THE MISANTHROPE was originally commissioned and produced by American Conservatory Theater, San Francisco CA. The play opened on 19 October 2000 with the following cast and creative contributors:

ALCESTE	David Adkins
PHILINTE	Gregory Wallace
ORONTE	Anthony Fusco
CÉLIMÈNE	René Augesen
ELIANTE	Kathleen Kaefer
ARSINOÉ	Kimberly King
ACASTE	Patrick McNulty
CLITANDRE	Chris Ferry
BASQUE	Steven Anthony Jones
DUBOIS/GUARD	David Mendelsohn
Ensemble	Darrick Clayton, Tom Clyde Meridith Crosley, Ian McConnel Eryka Raines, Paul Silverman
Director	Carey Perloff
Scenery	Kate Edmunds
Costumes	Beaver Bauer
Lighting	Rui Rita
Sound	Garth Hemphill
Dramaturg	Paul Walsh
Vocal coaching	Deborah Sussel
Movement staging	Francine Landes
Casting	Meryl Lind Shaw
Hair & makeup	Rick Echols
Associate director	Margo Whitcomb
Stage manager	Kimberly Mark Webb
Assistant stage manager	Elisa Guthertz
Intern stage manager	Elizabeth Murray

The workshop for this new verse version played in the Curtain Theater of the University of Massachusetts at Amherst, 18-21 October 2000. The cast and creative contributors were:

ALCESTE . . . . Robert K Wu*
PHILINTE . . . . .Michael D Walton
ORONTE . . . . .Joshua Boroff
CÉLIMÈNE . . . . Elaine Qualter
ELIANTE . . . . Dinora Walcott
ARSINOÉ . . . . Maya Sloan
ACASTE . . . . Nikita Anatoly Zaharov
CLITANDRE . . . . Eric S Cartier
BASQUE . . . . Meghan Anderson
DUBOIS . . . . Dan Smith
*Guest Artist

Director . . . . .Virginia Scott
Scenery . . . . .Louise Groll
Costumes . . . . June B Gaeke
Lighting . . . . .Melissa Mizell
Production manager . . . . .Catherine Bloch
Technical director . . . . Owen Reynolds

CHARACTERS & SETTING

ALCESTE, *in love with* CÉLIMÈNE
PHILINTE, ALCESTE's *friend*
ORONTE, *in love with* CÉLIMÈNE
CÉLIMÈNE, ALCESTE's *beloved*
ELIANTE, CÉLIMÈNE's *cousin*
ARSINOÉ, *a friend of* CÉLIMÈNE's
ACASTE, *a Marquess, suitor of* CÉLIMÈNE
CLITANDRE, *a Marquess, suitor of* CÉLIMÈNE
BASQUE, CÉLIMÈNE's *servant*
DUBOIS, ALCESTE's *valet*
GUARD *of the Marshals of France*

In and around CÉLIMÈNE's *house in Paris*

MOLIÈRE IN LOVE
Virginia Scott

The actor/playwright we know as Molière was born
Jean-Baptiste Poquelin in 1622 in Paris. His father was
a well-to-do merchant of beds and bedding who bought
for himself and his son the minor office of *tapissier*
(upholsterer) to the king. Jean-Baptiste was sent to the
most fashionable school in Paris and was destined for
the law, but all of M Poquelin's ambitious plans for his
son ended in January 1643, when Jean-Baptiste gave up
his right to succeed his father as royal *tapissier* and
joined with several other young people to found a
theater company.

Why would this carefully nurtured, well-educated
young bourgeois choose the unsubstantial and insecure
life of an actor? According to his colleague La Grange,
Molière "chose the profession from the invincible
inclination he had for the stage." And then, of course,
there was Madeleine.

Madeleine Béjart was older than Jean-Baptiste,
already an actress and a woman of considerable
experience in the *galanterie*, the world of rich men
and courtesans. Madeleine had glorious red hair.
She was elegant, witty, and a much-praised
tragedienne. On June 30, 1643, she, Jean-Baptiste, and
eight others founded the Illustrious Theatre; it wasn't.
After it failed, Madeleine and her lover, who had by
then taken the professional name of Molière, fled their
creditors and spent thirteen years touring the provinces.

Molière was in love with Madeleine. Unfortunately, that bare statement cannot be amplified. We do know that they lived together for a number of years, but never married. In the beginning Madeleine, who was professionally and sexually experienced, must have seemed exotic and powerful to her younger lover. As the years passed, however, Molière took the lead in the troupe, became its orator, its principal comic actor, and finally its playwright. The troupe did less and less tragedy. Madeleine grew older. The affair ended.

In the fall of 1658, the troupe returned to Paris. On January 23, 1662, a week after his fortieth birthday, Molière signed a marriage contract with another Béjart, Armande, aged "about twenty." Armande was either the daughter or the younger sister of Madeleine. The truth of her parentage has never been established, but she was raised within the troupe and Molière had known her all her life. It was not a successful union.

The year after the marriage, Molière wrote THE SCHOOL FOR WIVES, a comedy about a middle-aged man, Arnolphe, who has an obsessive fear of being cuckolded and so has never married. Instead, he has become guardian of a child, Agnès, whom he has had raised by nuns in total innocence and has retrieved from the convent to marry. Armande, of course, had been raised in anything but innocence by a company of actors. Nonetheless, the play caused a great scandal, because people assumed that Molière was writing about his own marriage. Seeing Agnès prepared to betray her ancient guardian with the handsome Horace, "all Paris" began to ask if Armande were still faithful to her husband.

Armande did not play Agnès. The first major role Molière wrote for his wife was the princess in a court entertainment entitled THE PRINCESS OF ELIS. The princess has three princely suitors, but swears she will never marry. Euryale, the prince of Ithaca, pretending to be even less interested in marriage, tells the lady that he is resolved never to fall in love. The princess says: "Without wanting to love, Seigneur, it is always very nice to be loved." The prince responds: "Madame, freedom is the goddess to whom I consecrate myself."

These lines may express the principal issues between Molière and Armande. Molière loved Armande, but Armande, while finding it "nice" to be loved, craved the freedom to live the life of a popular young actress. Molière had already exhibited his mixed feelings in THE SCHOOL FOR HUSBANDS, written six months before his wedding. Sganarelle and Ariste are brothers who, it might be argued, represent the playwright's own contradictory emotions. Sganarelle, jealous and possessive, refuses to let Isabelle, the young woman he wants to marry, leave his house. Ariste tries to talk his brother into being reasonable: "These bolts and these bars don't make a woman virtuous. Frankly, it would be a strange thing if a woman's honor depended only on constraint. I think that if you win her heart, she will protect her own honor and yours." But there precisely was the rub. In principle, Molière may have believed that marriage should not mean a circumscribed life for a woman, but there was a part of him that speaks through Sganarelle, Arnolphe, and, later, Alceste of his fear that he was not sufficiently lovable to win and keep the heart of the woman he loved.

Notorious "Autobiography"

Molière was a celebrity; the details of his conflict-ridden married life were a gossip's delight in his own time, spread through the seventeenth-century equivalents of supermarket tabloids. Some of what was written may be invention based on the plays; some of it may be imagined by the authors. Nonetheless, it gives Molière a voice worth hearing.

The most revealing account comes from a pamphlet attacking Armande entitled *The Infamous Actress*. In it

the anonymous author claims to have interviewed
Molière's dear friend Chapelle, which he may have
done. Chapelle certainly was Molière's closest friend,
and he was notoriously unable to keep what he knew to
himself. What "Chapelle" says is that he advised his
friend to have his unfaithful wife locked up as a
common whore. "Molière" answers:

> I can see you have never been in love. I was born
> deeply disposed to desire, and since, despite all
> my efforts, I have been unable to overcome this,
> I have tried to be as happy as one can be with such
> a susceptible heart.... My wife was very young when
> I married her, and I did not perceive in her any
> dishonorable inclinations...but I found that what
> she felt for me was far from what I needed in order
> to be happy. I did everything to conquer my
> feelings, since it was impossible to change them.
> I used all the strength of my spirit.... Now I am
> determined to live with her as if she were not my
> wife; but if you knew what I suffer, you would pity
> me.... You will doubtless say to me that it is mad to
> love like this. But I believe there is only one kind of
> love, and that people who have not felt this have not
> been in love at all.

In Grimarest's *Life of Molière*, a more self-critical
"Molière" speaks to another friend, Jacques Rohault:

> I only have what I deserve.... I believed my wife
> would adjust her behavior to my expectations,
> though I am well aware that if she had done so,
> she would be more unhappy than I am. She is lively,
> witty...she wants to enjoy her life, go her way.
> She knows she is innocent and she disdains the
> precautions I ask her to take. I conceive this neglect
> to be contempt. I need signs of her affection in order
> to believe that she has affection for me.

We know that Molière's marriage was troubled in the spring of 1666 when he was finishing THE MISANTHROPE. He had rented a small apartment in Auteuil, west of Paris, and was living there alone, recovering from a serious episode of tuberculosis. When the play opened on June 4, Molière played Alceste and Armande played Célimène. The audience on that opening night brought with them to the theater the scandal that circulated about the actor/playwright, as well as knowledge of his earlier plays about love and jealousy. Whether rightly or wrongly, Molière's private life was deeply implicated in their experience of the play.

It would, of course, be naive to assume that Molière's plays are simple autobiography, but equally naive to believe that Molière was a wholly objective writer who never used his feelings as a source for his theater. Molière's plays again and again project a complex and ambivalent attitude toward women, love, and marriage. A familiar argument is that a writer's work must be experienced entirely separately from his life. And, truly, the relationship of life and art is a difficult knot to untangle. But at the very least we can propose that, although Molière was not Alceste and Armande was not Célimène, had there been no Armande, had the marriage been other than it was, had Molière found happiness in love, there would be no MISANTHROPE.

Virginia Scott is the author of Molière: A Theatrical Life, *published in the United Kingdom by Cambridge University Press in September 2000.*

TRANSLATING MOLIÈRE

If you have seen THE MISANTHROPE before, you probably saw a translation written by Richard Wilbur. I am a big fan of Richard Wilbur and worked on a production of his translation of this play, directed by Mark Lamos, when I was on the artistic staff of the Hartford Stage Company in Connecticut. Mr Wilbur, single-handedly, brought the verse plays of Molière into the English-speaking canon, and his MISANTHROPE was the first of these that he finished. My translation is different because I made certain it was. But it would be different in some ways simply because I'm doing mine forty-seven years after his.

The language I chose for this version is slang-free, American English, typical of the latter half of the twentieth century. In some cases, I extended the comedy, but if it's really funny to you, it's probably Molière. I also clarified, and in some instances underscored, the many lawsuits and legal actions referred to in the play—at least that was my intention. Carey Perloff was fascinated by the amount of litigation that goes on in THE MISANTHROPE, an aspect of seventeenth-century social life not unlike our own and very important to understanding the forces at work on Célimène and Alceste.

Since I had done a translation of Molière's MISER for Hartford Stage, I was familiar with his commedia roots. My translation of Goldoni's SERVANT OF TWO MASTERS took me even closer to the Italian commedia

troupe that came to Paris and inspired much of
Molière's popular comedic style. But the characters in
THE MISANTHROPE are far beyond those familiar
commedia-based characters. Complex, intellectual,
completely three dimensional, all these people are very
current, and they certainly don't need to be "updated".
Yes, too, in writing THE MISANTHROPE Molière used
his feelings for his beautiful young wife, his connection
to the writing of a scandalous book, and the snubbing
and attacks he suffered for being an actor. But his
characters' concerns and their psychologies are
completely recognizable by almost anyone who
encounters this play, particularly urban dwellers and
anyone who works in a hierarchical system where the
power of favors, good opinion, and cadres makes
sincerity, spontaneity, and honesty difficult or even
dangerous to exercise. Only a "cameo" by DuBois,
Alceste's valet, reminds us where Molière's sensibility
as an actor was first formed. DuBois, like Goldoni's
Truffaldino, comes in like an old god, Pan or Kokopelli
or Anansi, to stir up chaos in this new world.

The Process

Now for some specifics in the process of translation.
My friend Virginia Scott, author of the new biography
Molière: A Theatrical Life, first created a seventy-one-
page literal, prose translation of the play from the
original French, with footnotes (134 of them!) about
variations in meaning, cultural and historical context,
etc. I then further translated her prose version into
iambic pentameter with rhyming couplets. Consider
these lines from one of Alceste's speeches in ACT ONE,
Scene One:

Scott's literal prose translation:

> I can't bear it any longer, I'm enraged, and my plan
> is to break with [or maybe "confront"] the whole
> human race.

Wilbur version:

> Ah, it's too much; mankind has grown so base,
> I mean to break with the whole human race.

Congdon version:

> And so I'll take an action even wiser,
> I'll break my lance on my opponent's visor,
> And go down fighting, face to bloody face,
> Then turn my back upon the human race.

In this particular case, I chose to take two couplets to express an idea that Wilbur translated in one line. Why? Because I was inspired, thanks to Virginia's footnote, by the French idiom used to express "confront" in the original: *"rompre en visière"*, which means "to break a lance in the enemy visor". I felt the extremity of action expressed by the idiom seemed an appropriate opportunity to show how intense and, at times, ridiculous Alceste becomes when he's emotional. Then Philinte's laughter, which follows this speech, is also more easily motivated. Philinte's lines clarify how this works:

Literal prose version:

> This philosophical gloom/melancholy is a little too savage (implication: uncivilized, antisocial). I laugh at these black outbursts when I contemplate you.

Wilbur version:

> This philosophic rage is a bit extreme;
> You've no idea how comical you seem.

Congdon version:

> The savage nature of your melancholy
> Just makes me laugh. You must perceive its folly.

These few examples can only begin to illustrate the function of choice in the translation process. Of course, the actor playing Philinte may choose not to laugh at

Alceste at this moment and, rather, do the line as if
Philinte were more derisive and sarcastic. Or the actor
may make a choice I haven't thought of.

About Character

The creation of a viable character onstage begins with
the text. Sometimes described and played as a "brittle
coquette", Célimène can become a cipher, but this
interpretation of her complex personality and
motivation hurts the dynamic of the play. I worked to
understand her and her situation and to make her as
intelligent and interesting as she was revealed to be in
the pages of Virginia's translation. I found Célimène's
voice to be surprisingly direct and honest, much more
like Eliante's than I had previously realized. She is a
good match for Alceste, in that they both have very
strong personalities. For a young woman of twenty,
I discovered her to be quite mature and savvy about
manipulating the world in which she lives. The
eventual failure of that manipulation is what makes
the play a dark comedy and the ending strangely
modern in its seriocomic tone.

And then there's Philinte, who is one of my favorite
characters in all of Molière's plays. Sometimes
interpreted as the *raisonneur*, a straightforward,
functional character who voices the standards of
thought and behavior of the author and the audience,
Philinte isn't always portrayed with the complexity and
reality that Molière originally gave him. He is a selfless,
long-suffering, good friend, like Horatio—a good
second fiddle who serves as ballast to Alceste's
outraged histrionics. And the modest and sweet way
in which he proposes to Eliante is very touching. But
the revelation of Philinte's casual misanthropy is one
of the great surprises of the play.

Working on a play so rich, so filled with wonderful
language and wit, and yet so economical in structure,
has been pure pleasure. Each act—there are five of

them—is rarely more than twenty minutes long.
In Molière's theater, twenty minutes was how long
the candles lasted before they had to be trimmed.
This ordinary fact of seventeenth-century theatrical
life bequeaths to us, a modern audience, a very tight
dramatic structure in which the action never stops
rolling. It's no wonder that Molière's brilliant social
satire has been adapted into other periods—
Hollywood, Paris under the rule of Charles de Gaulle,
Seattle's grunge culture. What I wonder is, Why adapt
it? To me, THE MISANTHROPE is perfectly current
in its concerns and in its characters—a twenty-first-
century play, a timeless play.

ACT ONE

Scene One

(ALCESTE *enters, angry.* PHILINTE *is right behind him.*)

PHILINTE: What's the matter?

ALCESTE: Just leave me alone.

PHILINTE: We're talking and you walk off. Now this "tone"?

ALCESTE: My tone is true, sir—more than I can say
About you, sir. Now, please just go away.

PHILINTE: This mood of yours, Alceste, is not endearing.
When you're like this, I can't get a fair hearing,
And I'm your oldest friend—

ALCESTE: My friend? Depart!
I claim no friend with a corrupted heart!

PHILINTE: Oh, here we go. Alceste, my friend, I see
I'm guilty of some misdeed, suddenly....

ALCESTE: After the hypocritical deceit,
That I just witnessed out there on the street,
When you encountered "whatshisname"—don't scoff,
I've only just begun to tell you off.
We meet him and you hug him like a brother!
And then inquire about his "lovely mother!"
Does he hear from her and is she well?
Hypocrisy enough right there for hell
To open up and take you down, but no,

You had many cloying words to go.
How's his "position" and is he "still—hmm—where?"
"Oh yes, that place," and is he "happy there?"
"Oh good!" You take his hand, look in his eyes.
It's what followed that made my gorge rise.

PHILINTE: What? He left. Without some farewell
"scene."

ALCESTE: After the farewell is what I mean.
I turned to you and simply asked, "Who's that?"
"Him? I'm not quite sure," is what came back.
"Is his mother lovely, too?" I said.
You didn't know. Now what if she'd been dead?
I wonder, then, yes? What would you have done?
Slobbered grief all over him, her son?
I hate to think, Philinte, how far you'd go.
"Integrity." Is that a word you know?
"Sincerity?" That's all I have to say.
I'd hang myself if I behaved that way.

PHILINTE: It hardly seems a hanging one—my crime.
I'll mitigate my sentence, this one time.

ALCESTE: Of course you'd make a joke, because you're
    blind
To the harm behavior of this kind
Visits on each person doing it.

PHILINTE: Since all of this is for my benefit—
Tell me, how would you, then, have me behave?
Respond to friendly greetings with a wave?
Pretend to be a mute? Or just be rude.

ALCESTE: Is it to my behavior you allude?
Yet, I am honest, sir, in all my dealings.

PHILINTE: At the sacrifice of people's feelings.
When a man approaches you with pleasure,
Should you not respond in equal measure?

Here's a coin of praise you give a friend—
And he returns in kind.

ALCESTE: Heaven forfend!
It's commerce, then! I understand it now.
There's a rate for praise and every vow.
I'll do this for you, and you for me,
I'll call you smart in your deep idiocy!
To hell with social commerce! It requires
That honest men must transform into liars.
How are we to live another hour,
In a world where pretense has such power?
You tell me, what merit has a man
Who praises you as highly as he can,
Who vows deep friendship, honoring you name,
Then turns to some scoundrel and says the same?
Would you agree, esteem implies a preference?
Yet with you, where is the point of reference?
If respect for merit you've relinquished,
Then choose me not—I want to be distinguished.
I'm sorry, but because you must pretend
To love mankind, then you are not my friend.

PHILINTE: But in polite society, which we are,
We follow rules of courtesy and, so far,
This custom has—

ALCESTE: —"This custom"—that's my point,
Is one that's wrenched our values out of joint.
The custom is to lie. Can you deny it?
You give up on the truth before you try it.
Vain compliments, pretended friendships—out!
Bring in an age of honesty, and shout,
"We are men and in all circumstance,
We speak from our hearts!" This is our stance,
Or should be now. It's not a lot to ask,
To live for truth and live without the mask.

PHILINTE: Living unmasked and with one's heart
  exposed

Seems much to ask. But what you have proposed
Could be construed as just a call for frankness,
But even that's ridiculous and thankless.
Would it be mannerly or à propos
To say to people everything you know,
Everything you think, every opinion?
Would chivalrous, white lies have no dominion?
Someone displeases you with what they wear,
Would you tell them the truth, right then and there?

ALCESTE: Yes.

PHILINTE: What? You would say to agéd Emily
That, even with the make up, she's no beauty?
In fact, the time has passed to look her best?

ALCESTE: I would.

PHILINTE: So you'd tell Dorilas, that pest,
That there is not an eardrum left unbattered
By his tall tales of family honor, spattered
With embellisments, beyond baroque?

ALCESTE: Of course I would.

PHILINTE: You're joking.

ALCESTE: I don't joke.
My eyes have suffered much—the court and town
Have carved onto this face a lasting frown.
And why? I see humanity's slow sink,
Into a world that's living on the brink,
Of total falsehood. Nothing's left but lies!
It's not enough to sit back and be wise,
When all I see is flattery so base,
Self-interest hid behind a caring face.
Injustice meets deception meets betrayal.
I've tried to compromise to no avail,
And so I'll take an action even wiser,
I'll break my lance on my opponent's visor,

And go down fighting, face to bloody face,
Then turn my back upon the human race.

PHILINTE: The savage nature of your melancholy
Just makes me laugh. You must perceive its folly.
I'm used to these black outbursts—we are brothers
Beneath the skin, beyond fathers and mothers.
There's this play, *The School for Husbands*, where—

ALCESTE: Literary references—unfair!
Stick to the point!

PHILINTE: If you will stop your rant,
And stop implying I'm a sycophant.
The world won't change because you say it must.
And since frankness is the only thing you trust,
I'll tell you, frankly, that this malady—
Disease of yours—results in comedy.
Yes, you're a comic figure in your wrath—
Poseidon roaring up from a birdbath.
Stick to the point? I shall and be meticulous.
People say your rages are ridiculous.

ALCESTE: So much the better! Now I know I'm right!
By god, I feel like dancing with delight.
To be seen as sane or sensible
By "people" would just be indefensible!

PHILINTE: No kind opinion for the human race?

ALCESTE: Not one that I can honestly embrace.

PHILINTE: So all mortals, all, without exception,
Are held by you in this same horrid perception?
Surely, in this century, there's some....

ALCESTE: I hate anything with an opposing thumb.
Some because they're wicked and pernicious.
Most for being lenient with the vicious,
Wrongly thinking tolerance will suffice
And not the hatred virtue owes to vice.
Leniency means license, yields injustice.

I'm being sued for nothing, yes? You know this.
And my litigant's a perfect scoundrel.
The nature of his character is known well.
His mask is downcast eyes, a honeyed tone.
Everyone we know seems to condone
The very shady way by which he's risen.
For me, I can't believe he's not in prison.
He's just some rustic clod, not from the city,
And yet he moves among the rich and witty.
The present splendour of his style of living
Has murdered any penchant for forgiving
I might have had. And what's worse, is this:
Call him villain, rogue or Beast from the Abyss,
And no one contradicts you! They agree!
By god, it wounds me more than mortally,
Death to my soul to see the way that vice
Is left to thrive, because we must be "nice."
Someday I'll leave for a deserted place,
And turn my back on the entire human race.

PHILINTE: Sometimes, there is no reason and no rhyme
To the agreed-on manners of the time.
Why not give human nature a reprieve?
We're not God casting Adam out with Eve.
Of course, I, too, see many things each day
That aren't as they should be, to my dismay.
And in each instance, I could show your rage,
But I don't do that. I accept this age.
I calmly try to take men as they are,
And banish judgment from my repertoire.
To see behavior in a kinder view
Is something I've accustomed my soul to.
And, although I know you don't agree,
My "niceties" are a philosophy—
As much an ethic as your attack on "fashion,"
Is my commitment to active compassion.

ALCESTE: But this compassion, sir, for which you speak,
Can nothing crack it, nothing make it weak?
What if a lover were to betray you?
Or a legal claim managed to waylay you?
Or some fool spread slander everywhere,
Against these, how would your compassion fare?

PHILINTE: Just fine, because of how I see mankind.
These vices, character defects, I find
Are part of human nature, and no different
Than wolves which we don't judge as belligerent,
Or vultures eating carrion as depraved,
Or apes or monkeys as badly behaved.
That's just how they are, that is their make-up.
From this utopian dream, you need to wake-up.

ALCESTE: So I'm to be betrayed, robbed, torn asunder,
And not be... Good God, the strain I'm under.
I can't talk about it anymore.

PHILINTE: That's good. Save it all for your solicitor.
Spend your effort on winning your lawsuit.

ALCESTE: I'm giving it no effort—that's absolute.

PHILINTE: But who is going to, then, take up your case?

ALCESTE: The firm of Reason, Equity and Justice is in
  place.
And, most of all, the rightness of my cause.

PHILINTE: Well, that's certainly a plan to give one pause.

ALCESTE: Is my case dubious, unjustifiable?

PHILINTE: No, but the rumor is you'll be found liable.

ALCESTE: I persist though I know I'm ill-fated.
I am either right or wrong—

PHILINTE: It's complicated.

ALCESTE: I shall not be moved.

PHILINTE: You may be moved.
Your opponent and his cadre—

ALCESTE: —will be disproved.

PHILINTE: As I said before: Alceste, awaken!

ALCESTE: You made it clear you think I am mistaken.

PHILINTE: I think you're doing something you'll regret.

ALCESTE: Losing the trial? No, I'll rejoice in that.

PHILINTE: Really, now—

ALCESTE: Yes, really, I will see,
If mankind has the effrontery,
To be that wicked, to be that perverse
To do me wrong before the universe.

PHILINTE: I give up.

ALCESTE: In fact, I'd like to lose it,
If the verdict's mine, I might refuse it.

PHILINTE: If people could hear you talk as you are now,
They'd laugh at you.

ALCESTE: And this affects me, how?

PHILINTE: Then I have to ask: This rectitude
That dominates your every attitude,
This honesty than which nothing matters more,
Do you find it in the one whom you adore?
I'm surprised, no, you astonish me.
Those very traits against which you admonish me,
Could be said to be a vital part
Of the one who captivates your heart.
Here you are, at war with the human race
Yet you lay down arms for this pretty face.
You know that Éliante is partial to you,
And as a person, she's sincere and true.
Arsinoé's a prude, but she's upright.
But neither of them blossom in your sight.

While Célimène, it seems, has all your heart,
And toys with it, with a coquettish art.
In the manners of the time, she's most adept.
Her gossip, even slander, you accept.
You hate the values she personifies,
Yet she's a perfect beauty in your eyes.
It's not as if she doesn't want to be them—
These things you hate. So do you just not see them?

ALCESTE: I think you're asking me, is my love "blind."
Let me assure you, it's nothing of the kind.
I know that this young widow has her faults,
And against them, I have launched assaults.
Whatever ardor she inspires in me
I condemn her weaknesses, loudly.
She has the art of pleasing me, somehow.
She makes me love her. Understand it now?
And without a doubt, I know my passion
Can cleanse her soul of all the sins of fashion.

PHILINTE: That will be no small accomplishment.
Does she love you? Are you confident?

ALCESTE: Of course she does. Are you on the attack?
I wouldn't love her, if she didn't love me back.

PHILINTE: You're sure her feelings for you dominate,
Yet rivals put you in a frenzied state.

ALCESTE: A heart like mine is conquered and not free,
So all I have is one sweet territory.
And I'm expected, placidly, to share it
With other men? I simply cannot bear it.
Today I've come to speak about that, only.
If I can't have her my way, I'll be lonely.

PHILINTE: If it were up to me, I know I'd want
To choose her pretty cousin, Éliante.
Her heart, that you esteem, is true, secure.
She only cares for you, you can be sure.

ALCESTE: I know. My reason tells me every day.
But reason can't rule love in any way.

PHILINTE: I fear the pain that you will undergo,
If—

Scene Two

(ORONTE, ALCESTE, PHILINTE)

ORONTE: *(To* ALCESTE*)*
They've gone shopping I was told below—
Éliante and her cousin Célimène.
When I found out that you were here, well, then,
I had to come and tell you, from my soul,
The respect I hold for you I give you whole.
It's grown so ardently, it has no end,
Except that you might number me a friend.
I dearly love to grant my recognition—
"Give merit where it's due," is my admission.
Because of my sincerity and station,
May I assume your heartfelt approbation?

(ALCESTE *doesn't seem to know that* ORONTE *is speaking to him.)*

ORONTE: What I said was for your ears intended.

ALCESTE: For me, sir?

ORONTE: Yes, you. You're not offended?

ALCESTE: No, but you do take me by surprise,
To know that I am honored in your eyes.

ORONTE: In the universe, honor most extreme,
Is what I give to you, with my esteem.

ALCESTE: Sir...

ORONTE: In all of France, no one aspires to
The worthiness one so admires in you.

ALCESTE: Sir...

ORONTE: I find you preferable, you see,
To all that of France has of nobility.

ALCESTE: Sir...

ORONTE: If I lie, may heaven crush me now!
And to confirm how deeply goes this vow,
Allow me to express this deepest friendship,
Embracing you as if we shared kinship.
Or, let's shake hands—if you prefer that way.
Friends for life!

ALCESTE: Sir...

ORONTE: What, then, do you say?

ALCESTE: Sir, I fear you honor me too much.
The wondrous mystery of friendship is such
That to use it often, as is your aim,
Surely would be to profane its name.
A union comes from intelligent choice,
And so, before we join hands and rejoice,
More about each other we should know,
Thus our natural reserve we can let go,
Allowing us to judge each other's actions
Before we enter into such transactions.

ORONTE: By god! Was there ever man more prudent?
And I, my friend, am your eternal student.
Well take time to form friendship's gentle bond,
Meanwhile, whatever you need, I'll wave my wand.
I have a certain credit with the king,
I have his ear and that's worth everything.
You still have my allegiance, you will find.
And since you have a most superior mind,
I'll launch this ship of trust we've just saluted
With this sonnet I just executed.
Is it good? As poetry, is it fit?
I want to know if I should publish it.

ALCESTE: Sir, I beg you, please, to pass me by.
I request a dispensation.

ORONTE: Why?

ALCESTE: My fault is my sincerity, I fear.

ORONTE: And for that reason I am glad I'm here.
Nothing less than truth or I will complain.
Don't spare me, no verbal legerdemaine.
To disguise your feelings is betrayal.

ALCESTE: What you desire, sir, must then prevail.

ORONTE: *Sonnet*... It's a sonnet. "Hope." It's written
For a lady with whom I am smitten.
"Hope..." This is not great verse from above
But rather little tender couplets of love.

ALCESTE: We will see.

ORONTE: "Hope..." I don't know if the style
Will seem naive and make you want to smile.
And if the word choice is too high or low.

ALCESTE: We will find that out.

ORONTE: Also, you should know,
I wrote it in a quarter of an hour.

ALCESTE: Just read it, sir, and we will judge its power.

ORONTE: *(Reads)* Hope, 'tis true, comforts us anon,
Puts roses in our cheeks when wan.
But, Philis, what a most sad benefit
When no thing hoped for follows after it.

PHILINTE: I'm charmed by its simple eloquence.

ALCESTE: How brilliant would it be if it made sense?

ORONTE: Your constant kindnesses end our ennui,
But would that you were more miserly,
Not given to such generous expenditure,
Dear Philis, of hope, then better we'd endure.

PHILINTE: Ah, the elegance of mood and turn of phrase!

ALCESTE: How low you sink, Philinte, for heights of praise!

ORONTE: If it should be that this eternal waiting,
Prolongs my zealous ardor to my death,
Then zealot shall I be, with my last breath.

Your little favors, Philis, won't appease me,
Beautiful Philis, receive me e'er I mope,
Because I'm in despair with joyful hope.

PHILINTE: Oh, that ending is admirably amorous and deep.

ALCESTE: You sound just like him! Stop it! I could weep.

PHILINTE: Have I heard better verses? I think not.

ALCESTE: Oh god.

ORONTE: You flatter me.

ALCESTE: It's total rot!

PHILINTE: Not flattery at all—

ALCESTE: Oh, let this end!

ORONTE: (To ALCESTE)
Remember our agreement, as my friend:
Complete sincerity, exactly what you think.
Can hardly wait—I'm trembling on the brink.
Your utmost candid thoughts are what I seek.

ALCESTE: It's delicate, this business of critique.
Everyone wants praise and nice attention.
The other day, to someone I won't mention,
I said, after he read his sonnet—whole—
That gentlemen must practice self-control.
When the urge arises to write something
It doesn't hurt to give your head a thumping.
Remind yourself to hold on to that treasure.
Don't show what you have written for your pleasure.

I told this "man" to keep in mind this rule,
"He who *plays* at poetry, plays a fool."

ORONTE: Let me be clear on what you're trying to say,
I am wrong to want to—

ALCESTE: —write this way?
What I said to "him" was that bad writing
Gives one's friends a reason for back-biting.
A man may have a coat with medals on it—
At death he'll be interred *in* his bad sonnet.

PHILINTE: But with your poem, I find that I'm quite
smitten.

ORONTE: Are you finding fault with what I've written?

ALCESTE: I don't say that, but to save my friend,
I pointed out how good careers can end.
This thirst for verse has ended lives quite sadly.

ORONTE: Am I like them? Do you think that I write
badly?

ALCESTE: I don't say that, but I said this to him,
Why write? Why rhyme? Admit it's just a whim.
A noxious whim at that, to be resisted!
Don't follow all the morons who persisted!
The publishing of a bad book is forgiven,
Writers have habits and they're very driven.
And no one stops them or they need the money.
Some avaricious printer thinks it's funny.
The book comes out—respect's a dying ember.
The readers hate you, beg you to remember
That when you're writing something rich and fulgent,
What's on the page is often self indulgent.
When next you want to write, sit on your hand!
I tried in vain to make *him* understand.

ORONTE: Back to my sonnet—from you, could I hear
more?

ALCESTE: Put this sonnet deep inside a drawer.
You've followed to a "T" the bad examples.
Just listen as I catalog the samples.

"Hope comforts us anon." Now that is treason.
I know it rhymed with "wan," but that's the reason?

"But, Philis, what a most sad benefit
When no thing hoped for follows after it."
What?

"Your little favors, Philis, won't appease."
That line's so bad it brings me to my knees.

"Beautiful Philis, receive me e'er I mope."

This kind of writing is a slippery slope.
Because this style embodies good intentions,
The road to hell is paved with its inventions.
I fear the turn of phrase which pleases you,
Is so far from the natural and the true,
It's nothing but word play, pure affectation.
To understand it, I need a translation.
I could not tell what you were trying to say.
In the real world no one talks that way!
The bad taste of our time is very frightening.
I keep praying for a bolt of lightning
To hit some poet as he invokes his muse,
Leaving behind only his smoldering shoes.
Our fathers, yes, had much better taste.
Crude they were, but let me say with haste,
They recognized and valued what was true.
Like this old song I'm going to sing to you:
(He sings.)
If the King had offered me
Paris, his great home
And for it asked me to leave
My true love alone
I would say to King Henri
You take back your great Paree,

I love my darling more, I do,
I love my darling more.

The rhyme's not rich, the style's old-fashioned,
But can't you hear, the sentiment's impassioned.
(He speaks it.)
If the King had offered me
Paris, his great home
And for it asked me to leave
My true love alone
I would say to the King Henri
You take back your great Paree,
I love my darling more, I do,
I love my darling more.

Now that is how a man in love would speak.
(To PHILINTE *who is laughing)*
You laugh. But listen now to my critique:
This simple poem, indeed, a children's song,
Free of glossy rhyme schemes, not very long,
Is more truthful and more admired by me
Than some "sonnet" rife with pomposity.

ORONTE: And I maintain my verses are quite good.

ALCESTE: You have your reasons, yes, of course you
would.
I'll never like your verse, that's evident.
I have my reasons, too. Now, be content.

ORONTE: It's enough to know that others praise them.

ALCESTE: Apparently bad verse just doesn't faze them.
Or they have learned the art of faking it.

ORONTE: You think you have more than your share of
wit.

ALCESTE: To praise your verse, I'd need more than that.
But I won't lie and I'm no diplomat.

ORONTE: I'll get along without your approbation.

ALCESTE: Do that, then, and without hesitation.

ORONTE: One wonders, on this subject, what you'd
  write
With your superior taste.

ALCESTE: Indeed, I might.
And, by mischance, write something badly done,
But I would not be showing everyone.

ORONTE: Your arrogance only exceeds your vanity.

ALCESTE: Your need for praise reaches insanity.

PHILINTE: My friends, it's taste you're putting to the
  test—
De gustibus non disputantem est.

ORONTE: Look here, you *nobody*, I'd watch my tone.

ALCESTE: And who are you? You'd better watch your
own.

PHILINTE: *(Coming between them)*
I beg you to stop with all my heart!
And apologize, please.

ORONTE: I must depart.
I am sorry, sir. My apology I gave.

ALCESTE: And I accept it, as your humble slave.

(Exit ORONTE*)*

Scene Three

(PHILINTE, ALCESTE)

PHILINTE: And isn't this just fine! You were sincere!
And now you have a problem that's severe.
All Oronte wanted was to be flattered
But you held your ground, as if it mattered.

ALCESTE: No more talking.

PHILINTE: But...

ALCESTE: No more company.

PHILINTE: Come now—

ALCESTE: Leave me!

PHILINTE: If...

ALCESTE: Do not speak to me!

PHILINTE: You're....

ALCESTE: Not listening.

PHILINTE: But...

ALCESTE: You can't hear me?

PHILINTE: What did I...?

ALCESTE: By god, do not come near me.

PHILINTE: Why insult me, when...

ALCESTE: I look, I find you!

PHILINTE: That's right. Wherever you are, I'm there, too!

ALCESTE: Why don't you leave? What is it that you want?

PHILINTE: Someone should go and fix things with Oronte.

END OF ACT ONE

ACT TWO

Scene One

ALCESTE: Célimène, I'm going to speak bluntly.
The way that you behave enrages me.
The end is clear, so why prolong the wait.
In my mind, we should simply separate.
I could tell you that it's not a fact,
But I'd be lying, and I don't do that.
Although a million times, I'd promise you
That we could stay together, it's not true.

CÉLIMÈNE: You waited for me here, but now I see,
Your principal desire was to scold me.

ALCESTE: I don't scold and that isn't my intent.
Besides, we're speaking of *your* temperament.
Your nature is to litter up the floor
With anyone who knocks upon your door.
Admirers are prowling everywhere!
And that's too much for this true heart to bear.

CÉLIMÈNE: Your problem is the men you claim to be
"Littering" my life with love for me?
So I'm to forbid men to find me charming,
Because the number of them you find so alarming.
They come to call so nicely every day,
But I'm to take a stick, chase them away!

ALCESTE: Célimène, there's no necessity for a stick.
I only ask your heart to be less quick
In welcoming each male that you attract.

I've had to accept this very obvious fact:
Your beauty is innate, it's captivating,
Because of this, there are many captives waiting,
And they cherish these chains because you're sweet
And always nice to them, here, in the street,
Wherever you see them, it doesn't matter,
You entertain them with your obliging chatter.
You say their joyful hope has no basis.
I wish they knew that. I'm tired of their faces.
And this Clitandre—I don't understand,
What's the attraction? Have you seen his hand?
His little finger has a nail this long.
Think of the many doors he's scratched upon
To gain some entry. You expect my wrath?
No, but it does make me want to take a bath.
Is it his costume that you like the most?
I know he does, he's ever wont to boast.
Or is it that he's your devoted slave?
Unmanly, and an odious way to behave.

CÉLIMÈNE: How unjust of you to take offense!
He's promised his support for my defense.
Yours is not the only legal fight.
I have a lawsuit, too, that must end right.

ALCESTE: Lose your lawsuit, keep your integrity—
Don't indulge this rival who offends me.

CÉLIMÈNE: Just when I think it can't get any worse,
You become jealous of the universe.

ALCESTE: The universe, itself, was just a place
Until you welcomed it in your embrace.

CÉLIMÈNE: This tendency of mine should calm your heart,
My affectionate attention, I impart
Impartially, like water that just flows
And is diluted everywhere it goes.

If one particular person I befriended,
You might have reason, then, to be offended.

ALCESTE: What do I have, then, that the others don't?
Forget the jealousy, you say. I won't.
What's the gift for me they don't have, too?

CÉLIMÈNE: The happiness of knowing I love you.

ALCESTE: How can I believe that that is true?

CÉLIMÈNE: Because I take the risk of telling you.
Like all women, I am loathe to state
My deepest feelings, and I hesitate.
So my direct admission is a prize.

ALCESTE: How can I be sure it's not a guise?
What if this is a rehearsed repeat
Of a common scene with men—

CÉLIMÈNE: How sweet!
And from a lover, what a compliment!
Sweet "nothings," to be sure, and cruelly meant.
How much integrity you see in me!
Well, I'll relieve your deep anxiety.
I take back each syllable I spoke,
And every bit of feeling I revoke.
You're safe from any ardor that might warm you.
You want to see the person who can harm you?
Look in the mirror. See that scowling face?
There's your deceiver, the source of your disgrace.

ALCESTE: My god! Why do I love you so? It's mad!
Loving someone else would not be bad,
If only I could do it. Desire, depart!
How did you get your hands around my heart?
I'd fall down on my knees and bless the skies,
If one day this outrageous love just dies.
I know that I've done everything I can:
"Get over it! Behave like a man!"

I've even prayed, but silence from above!
It must be for my sins that I'm in love!

CÉLIMÈNE: As a declaration of love, that is unique.

ALCESTE: Your capture of my heart has made me weak.
My love is past conceiving and no one
Has ever loved as I do—to oblivion.

CÉLIMÈNE: And this is love? My god, you're such a
    martyr
To this union of anger and ardor.
Chastening as wooing just won't do.
I respond to kinder words from you.

ALCESTE: And kinder words will come if you will
    change.
But, please, let's end this frustrating exchange,
And speak with open hearts and stop—

(BASQUE *enters.*)

CÉLIMÈNE: Yes, Basque?

BASQUE: Acaste is here.

CÉLIMÈNE: I have to see Acaste.

ALCESTE: We never have a moment's rest alone!
Must you insist on running a salon?

CÉLIMÈNE: Would you rather I insult, ignore him?
He knows I'm home and waiting would just bore him.

ALCESTE: "Boring Acaste"—not much of a vice.
But as description, it is very nice.

CÉLIMÈNE: Good lord! The good will of such people
    matters!
You're thinking, "Oh, another one she flatters."
You're right and I will do it yet again.
I need to stay on the good side of men
Who've won the right to speak out at the court.
Don't look at me like that, Alceste, and snort.

They've won this right by being politic,
A skill you don't respect—

ALCESTE: It makes me sick.

CÉLIMÈNE: From a truly honest stance they can't divert
    you.
But though they never help you, they can hurt you.

ALCESTE: So, in the end, whoever comes to visit.
Regardless of their reason, you're complicit
And willing to extend your tolerance.
Is anyone unwelcome here, perchance?

BASQUE: Clitandre's here, again. Pardon.

ALCESTE: Of course.
I look at you and don't see one sign of remorse.

I have to leave!

CÉLIMÈNE: Please stay.

ALCESTE: Oh, why should I?

CÉLIMÈNE: I want you to.

ALCESTE: I won't.

CÉLIMÈNE: Don't say good-bye.

ALCESTE: To your character, these gatherings are
    injurious,
And, besides, you know they make me furious.

CÉLIMÈNE: But I want you to, I want you to—just stay.

ALCESTE: Impossible! Don't ask!

CÉLIMÈNE: Then go away!!

Scene Two

(ÉLIANTE, PHILANTE, ACASTE, CLITANDRE, ALCESTE,
CÉLIMÈNE, BASQUE)

ÉLIANTE: *(To* CÉLIMÈNE)
Two gentlemen are on the stairs below.
They're waiting there, or did you just not know?

CÉLIMÈNE: I knew. And Basque, bring chairs for
  everyone.
(To ALCESTE)
You haven't gone?

ALCESTE: No. I want something done.
To them or me, I want you to commit.

CÉLIMÈNE: Be quiet.

ALCESTE: Today, it must be definite.

CÉLIMÈNE: You have lost your mind.

ALCESTE: I've become sane.

CÉLIMÈNE: I don't think so.

ALCESTE: Must I ask again?
I will. Please choose now, is it them or me?

CÉLIMÈNE: Alceste, this is complete insanity.

ALCESTE: No, it's not. This is the moment. Choose.

CLITANDRE: Dear God! The Louvre—what an unfit
  place to lose
One's temper, and about "inappropriate" adorning.
And yet, that's what Cleonte did just this morning.
As usual, all of us had outdressed him
So he began to rail, it so distressed him.
Has he no friend who could take him aside,
And say, "Stop these tirades no one can abide?"

CÉLIMÈNE: It's true. His image in society is tarnished.
But a bad painting can't be changed once varnished.
And every time you see him, don't you find?
He seems more and more out of his mind?

ACASTE: Dear God! The sane ones, if they have a mind
   to,
Can bore you dead, if only they can find you.
Damon trapped me today, in the hot sun.
Although I tried to run and hide, he won.

CÉLIMÈNE: He tirelessly holds forth, it's quite amazing.
Says nothing, and repeats it, paraphrasing,
Proceeds to more "nothing," yet words still flow.
The next time, do what I do—fake vertigo.

ÉLIANTE: *(To* PHILANTE*)*
That was just the heat to qualify,
Now comes the race—just watch the gossip fly.

CLITANDRE: A painting that's performed with verbal
   pen:
"A Portrait of Timante," by Célimène.

CÉLIMÈNE: From head to toe, a total man of mystery
Whose legacy, to him, is part of history.
Who has no business, yet is always busy.
If you asked, someone would say, "Who is he?"
And yet, he views each hour like a spy,
In glances from the corner of his eye.
He waits 'til you are speaking, then he walks
Sideways, like a crab, and when he talks,
It's *entre nous*, and sad, as if you're lonely,
And a "secret", but for your ears only.
Of course, the secret always is mundane.
But, to him, it's knowledge most arcane.
He even starts the day with an ominous warning,
By oozing up to you and whispering, "Good morning."

ACASTE: And Geralde?

ÉLIANTE: Oh, let the games begin!

CÉLIMÈNE: He's always going somewhere with his chin.
Having left a most important meeting,
He barely has the breath for a proper greeting.
And, besides, he's not certain of your name
Because you just don't possess—well, you know, fame.
You see, his day is spent only with princes.
Time with us? He can't see what the sense is.
Princes and dukes and all nobility
Grant him this life of great mobility.
They hunt with him and share his dogs and horses.
He's intimate with many powerful forces.
But when they're out in public, and he's near,
They don't seem to hold him quite as dear.

CLITANDRE: But with Belise, he's on the best of terms.

CÉLIMÈNE: She's so boring, she is like the worms
That bore into a piece of wood, so slightly.
That one tends to take her much too lightly.
But, literally, she's bored people to tears—
The result of open yawning to their ears.
Yes, you do it now. Down to your chins!
Mere mention of her name, and it begins.
She bores holes into my brain with every visit:
"The weather seems quite pleasant now, or is it?"
I hear myself, but in my martyrdom
I'm paralyzed, and so I start to hum.
If I didn't lie to leave the room,
I think she'd stay until the Crack of Doom.
In fact, without those little lies, my dear,
I can guarantee she'd still be here.

ACASTE: How does Adraste strike you?

CÉLIMÈNE: He should be struck!
And quickly, too. Or by a rapier stuck.
A fitting judgment for that rank buffoon,
Who wouldn't bleed—he's like a big balloon.

A little prick and he'd be liberated,
Emitting air until he was deflated.
No damage would be done, he'd be just fine.
Although he would be jealous and would whine,
Because someone he knows was hit headlong,
And flew around the room, for twice as long.

CLITANDRE: This young Cleon—that is his name,
   I think?
Plies aristocrats with food and drink.
His house, they say, is stacked right to the roof
With the pretentious and the most aloof.

CÉLIMÈNE: His house would never get a second look
If it weren't for the genius of his cook.

ÉLIANTE: His meals, though—they are the most refined.

CÉLIMÈNE: But on his personality I've dined.
If he'd listen, I'd make this suggestion:
Serve less of yourself to aid digestion.
Spending time with him, less than an hour,
Can make the sweetest *bombe glace* taste sour.

PHILINTE: His Uncle Damis everyone commends,
Do you like him?

CÉLIMÈNE: He's one of my friends.

PHILINTE: A well-bred man, temperate and sensible.

CÉLIMÈNE: But his mannered speech is indefensible!
The hours he spends at home, practicing *bon mots*,
So he can drop them everywhere he goes!
And from his first word, he points up with haste
The enviable elevation of his taste.
Everything he reads, he finds unfit,
Because praise isn't worthy of a wit.
He got into his head, "I must be clever."
And all his wit goes into that endeavor.
Finding fault is a mark of learning,
Enjoying something is just not discerning.

He thinks that only fools applaud and laugh,
And loving what you see—an awful gaff.
By standing on all those he finds inferior,
He elevates himself to the superior.

ACASTE: *(To* CÉLIMÈNE*)*
That portrait is so perfect he could sue.

CLITANDRE: No one can paint character like you.

ALCESTE: Cut and thrust, like the good courtiers you are!
You spare no one, but, look, the door's ajar!
All of them are coming into view!
Your parries become bows, you kiss and coo,
Swear loyalty—

CLITANDRE: You're blaming us? For witticisms?
To Célimène address your criticisms.

ALCESTE: Good lord! It's you and your indulgent
   laughter
That give her just the audience she's after!
Her aptitude for mocking's nicely nourished,
And with your tending, it has really flourished.
Not blame you for her obvious lack of feeling?
Why else would malice, to her, be appealing?

PHILINTE: You care about these people "at the door?"
You would condemn what she just chides them for.

CÉLIMÈNE: Of course, the gentleman contradicts like
   this.
You know he only loves antithesis.
The issue could be profane or be ethical,
He'll take whatever side is antithetical.
You see, he would be seen as commonplace
If he returned the smile on someone's face
And agreed with them, just to be nice.
Not to contradict's the only vice.
His own beliefs, ideas he holds true?
If someone else should voice them, he'll argue.

Like a lawyer, he'll construct a brief
To press a claim against his own belief!

ALCESTE: Go on, continue with this caricature.
God knows, they find it funny, to be sure.

PHILINTE: Whatever people say, and this is true,
Is unacceptable and angers you.
The fact that you can't swallow blame or praise
Sets you apart from people in all ways.

ALCESTE: My anger's righteous—that's the point,
    Philinte.
The human race is wrong—I won't recant—
Because whatever people say to me
Is couched in such extreme hyperbole,
Unmerited praise or complete condemnation,
And you know how much I value moderation.
Is it any wonder no one's right?
I see my righteous anger as a light
Diogenes would carry in his hand,
To search the world for just one honest man.

CÉLIMÈNE: But—

ALCESTE: No, strike me dead for saying it here:
This parlor game of yours offends my ear.
The pleasure that you take in what I hate,
I can't bring myself to even tolerate.

CLITANDRE: Until this moment, I just have to say,
I thought her consummate in every way.

ACASTE: That she is less than charming is just risible.
And any faults she has must not be visible.

ALCESTE: They're visible to me and I deplore them,
She knows that I take pains not to ignore them.
There's great discernment in a lover's gaze
That doesn't flatter, doesn't lay on praise.
If I were her, I'd never trust a man
Who defers to me every time he can,

And I would banish all the men who pander
And indulge me in my joy of slander.

CÉLIMÈNE: So, a true lover, as defined by you,
All endearments, tributes he'd eschew,
And he and his true love would spend their days
Murmuring rebukes instead of praise.

ÉLIANTE: But I thought lovers acted otherwise,
And rarely found a thing to criticize.
Don't lovers always praise the one they choose?
"Discernment" is the first thing that they lose.
They're blind to things they normally would blame,
And if "discerned," they use another name.
If she's pale, she's as white as jasmine,
If she's swarthy, she's kissed by the sun,
If she's skinny, she is lithe and graceful,
If she's fat, she's a healthy one,
If she's a slattern, she's a negligent beauty,
If she's a giant, with goddesses she'll run,
If she's a dwarf, she's a petite marvel,
If she's haughty, she's a phenomenon,
The deceiver's clever, and the fool is virtuous,
The chatterbox is such a lot of fun,
The mute one's deep, the shy one's choosy,
Thus lovers can be in love with anyone.

ALCESTE: I still insist—

CÉLIMÈNE: How lovely it would be
To take a turn around the gallery.
You're not leaving, gentlemen?

CLITANDRE: No.

ACASTE: No.

ALCESTE: You seem to be afraid that they might go.
Leave when you like, my friends, but I warn you,
I'm not leaving until after you do.

ACASTE: Today? I haven't any special thing.

CLITANDRE: Nor I—until the bedtime of the king.

CÉLIMÈNE: *(To* ALCESTE*)*
I assume you're being funny.

ALCESTE: Not today.
We'll just see who it is you want to stay.

Scene Three

*(*BASQUE, ALCESTE, CÉLIMÈNE, ÉLIANTE, ACASTE,
PHILINTE, CLITANDRE*)*

BASQUE: *(To* ALCESTE*)*
Sir, some men are here who told me to say
They have to speak to you without delay.

ALCESTE: I have no urgent business. Tell them no.

BASQUE: They're dressed officially, from top to toe.

CÉLIMÈNE: Go see who it is, or bring them here.

*(*GUARD *enters.)*

ALCESTE: *(To the* GUARD*)* What is it you want?

GUARD: This in your ear:
The Marshalls of France, whose commands we bear,
Have summoned you before them. Please prepare.

ALCESTE: Who me?

GUARD: You, sir.

ALCESTE: Whatever do they want?

PHILINTE: *(To* ALCESTE*)*
You know that it's your squabble with Oronte.

CÉLIMÈNE: *(To* PHILINTE*)* What's this?

PHILINTE: *(To* CÉLIMÈNE*)*
Oronte composed and read a sonnet,
Sought Alceste's candid opinion on it.

The city police, fearing a duel,
Have now intervened.

CÉLIMÈNE: *(Alarmed, worried for* ALCESTE*)*
He's such a fool!

ALCESTE: When will the judges rule on this? Posthaste?
And they dare to condemn me for my *taste*?
If, to settle this, I must retract,
That won't happen, nor would it change this fact:
The sonnet is *execrable*,

PHILINTE: Don't make it worse.

ALCESTE: And not a sonnet. No, it's barely verse.

PHILINTE: If you could just be more accommodating,
And berate a little less...

ALCESTE: Who's berating?
Unless His Majesty the King asks me today,
To approve these verses central to this fray,
I will maintain their total lack of worth,
And that their author be banished from the earth.
(To CLITANDRE *and* ACASTE*)*
You're laughing at me, sir and sir, it's clear.

CÉLIMÈNE: Wherever you've been summoned, do appear.

ALCESTE: I go, but I'll return and when I am through,
We will settle who I am to you.

END OF ACT TWO

ACT THREE

Scene One

(CLITANDRE, ACASTE)

CLITANDRE: My dear Acaste, why are you so content?
Nothing bothers you, you're cheerful, confident.
What reason could you have, that you'd confide,
To be so totally self-satisfied?

ACASTE: Good lord! Look at me! I can say with pride,
Of course, I'm nothing less than satisfied.
I'm young. I'm rich. I own property.
My family's bloodline is of real nobility.
The King is pleased with me, and before long,
I'll get some royal post that comes along.
And when the subject's courage, people tell
How on the field of honor, I excel.
And, even more, it's said that I compete
With a steady hand and nimble feet.
I'm intelligent—that is understood,
And it's known my taste is more than good.
All look to me because, without reflection,
I can see an object's imperfection,
And simply, judge a thing right on the spot,
And tell you if it's good or if it's not.
I love the theater, and sit up on the stage,
Where my reaction can serve as a gauge:
I lead the crowd in hisses and bravos
So, based on my response, a play might close.
I am handsome. My teeth are sound and white.

I've been told my laugh is a delight.
My figure's good, my waist is fairly small,
It's said my graceful walk is watched by all.
Am I well-dressed? Observe. I rest my case.
As to the fairer sex. I'll say with grace,
I'm successful. So, forgive my pride—
With all this, a man is satisfied.

CLITANDRE: Since easy conquest is your true domain,
Why linger here quite obviously, in vain?

ACASTE: In vain, you say? Do I look like a man
Who "lingers" anywhere, in the hope he can
Receive some favor from some frigid beauty
Like those who wrongly think it is their duty,
As gentlemen-to-be, to suffer anguish,
So, for love, of course, they have to languish.
Those without the in-born social graces
Are often found lingering in places
Where they'll never have the least success.
One wonders why they stay? I cannot guess.
But my class of person is not meant
To wallow in the mire of languishment,
Behaving like a slave, trying to inherit
A love we'd quickly claim with our own merit.
To spend my love, so obviously a prize,
On hopes, would be unseemly and unwise.

CLITANDRE: If I may clarify, you think she favors you?

ACASTE: I have my reasons, friend, to think that's true.

CLITANDRE: If that is what you think, friend, you are
    blind,
You're self-deluded and out of your mind.

ACASTE: Oh yes, I'm self-deluded, blind and—what—
    insane?

CLITANDRE: What makes you think that you've won
    this campaign?

ACASTE: Delusion.

CLITANDRE: What are you using as a base?

ACASTE: Insanity.

CLITANDRE: Just tell me to my face.

ACASTE: But I can't see you, friend, because I'm blind,
And worse than that, I am out of my mind.

CLITANDRE: Have you acquired favor with Célimène?

ACASTE: No, she hates me.

CLITANDRE: Tell the truth. I ask again.

ACASTE: But I'm deluded.

CLITANDRE: All right! Just stop, please!
Reason for hope from her? Or all a tease?

ACASTE: The truth, my friend, is you're the lucky one.
On you, doth rise the moon and set the sun.
In fact, I know you are her heart's delight.
And so, I'm going to hang myself tonight.

CLITANDRE: Enough! Let's bring this quarrel to an end,
And make a solemn pact, just friend to friend,
If either of us has real evidence,
That he is favored in a valid sense,
The other must give up, give way, and yield,
And to the victor will belong the field.

ACASTE: All right, by god, to that I will agree,
With all my heart, my friend, and so we'll see....
But hush!

Scene Two

(CÉLIMÈNE, ACASTE, CLITANDRE)

CÉLIMÈNE: Still here?

ACASTE: In love we do abide.

CÉLIMÈNE: I just heard a carriage stop outside.
Who could it be?

Scene Three

(BASQUE, CÉLIMÈNE, ACASTE, CLITANDRE)

BASQUE: Arsinoé is here,
And sends her love.

CÉLIMÈNE: As always, so sincere.

BASQUE: She's chatting now downstairs with Éliante.

CÉLIMÈNE: "Chatting?" Lord, what does the creature
want?

CLITANDRE: You have a visit from the consummate
   prude.
Oh, lucky you—

CÉLIMÈNE: I guess I can't be rude.

ACASTE: The fervor of her zeal—

CÉLIMÈNE: —is such a bore,
Especially since it's fake right to its core.
She's just as worldly as either one of you!
To hook a man is all she wants to do.
But having no luck, she's always jealous,
And so about morality, she's zealous.
Other people's charms must be a sin,
Because her own are gone, to her chagrin.
And since her agéd looks can't be the rage,
She rails against the blindness of this age.
Because no man will come into her arms,
She makes a crime of other people's charms.
In point of fact, of course, she's very lonely,
But upon Alceste she's focused, only.
She thinks that I have stolen him from her.
It's a delusion she will not abjure.

Her jealous spite is unleashed everywhere
Against me. It's so stupid. I don't care.
I wish that I could make her go away,
Take her foolishness and—

Scene Four

(ARSINOÉ *enters.* CÉLIMÈNE, ACASTE, CLITANDRE)

CÉLIMÈNE: Arsinoé!
Oh, what happy fate has brought you here.

ARSINOÉ: The truth? I've been worried about you, dear.
I've come to caution; others just condemn.

CÉLIMÈNE: Shall we sit down?

ARSINOÉ: I'd rather not. And them?

CÉLIMÈNE: They're leaving.

(CÉLIMÈNE *gives the men a look and the men exit, trying to hold back their laughter.*)

CÉLIMÈNE: Gone.

ARSINOÉ: That's very good you know.
Their departure's very apropos.
What I have to say, and I'll be brief,
Centers on a deeply held belief:
A friend should be a, sort of, moral signpost,
For the things that, to us, matter most.
Nothing matters more than reputation.
Yesterday, I made a visitation
To the home of people of great virtue.
The way your name was mentioned would have hurt
    you.
Proper behavior for one's age and station
Was the focus of the conversation.
Your behavior, which was the question raised,
Had the misfortune of not being praised.

What I'm saying, Célimène, please hear
In the spirit that it's given, dear.
The many, many men who visit you—
Alarming in the number of them, true?—
Have made some vocal citizens conclude
That they, the men, are here for something rude
(You agree, it has to be admitted,
There are some things that cannot be permitted),
"Activities" you'd blush at, were they named.
And then, your flirty ways, have to be blamed
For this portrait which I'm painting here
Of Célimène, the Jade, or something near.
I, your friend, at every turn, defended
What I could, until I was quite winded.
I'm sure you're most upset. I know I'd be
If I thought the world thought thus of me.
So, my advice to you? My dear? Be careful.
No need to thank me—just a friendly earful.

CÉLIMÈNE: I wasn't going to thank you, there's no need.
I know your visit here is a good deed.
And out of friendship, I'll return the favor,
And tell you how you're seen, so we can savor
This sweet moment, free of acrimony.
So here's the truth: most people think you're phony.
I don't know why. But this is what I hear.
They say appearances are all that you hold dear,
And that face of pious indignation
Barely hides your sexual frustration.
I have to say, your walk, that is, your carriage,
Has the swing of someone wanting marriage,
But letting envy, anger, judgment, fear
Repel even a desperate man who's near.

But I digress, my opinions do not matter.
We're friends, my friend, so I don't need to flatter.
It's what society at large says, isn't it?
And what they say is, "She's a hypocrite."

No, no, don't thank me, I have more to share.
My raison d'etre, dear, is your welfare.
Now where was I? Oh yes. What people say
When they talk about you—*every* day.
You cheat your servants and hide bills you owe.
Well, I said you had stopped that long ago.
(And other things they said were outright slander.)
About your make-up—you might take a gander
At the clown face you've got going there.
But I don't blame you, age is hard to bear.

ARSINOÉ: So I have made you angry, that is clear.
But I shall take the high road, yes, my dear.
My staying through your onslaught may seem weak—
But I have learned to turn the other cheek.

CÉLIMÈNE: I'm not angry. I think it's sensible.
To resist true honesty is indefensible.
I'm thinking—yes? That we should meet more often,
And voice these "honesties" before we soften
Them with niceties. And we turn meek
And hesitant. I say we meet next week.
Am I free? Do I have a reception?
I'll clear the day. To conquer self-deception
Is more important than any herd of men
I might be seeing. You'll come back again?

ARSINOÉ: "Come back again?" I doubt I'm welcome,
    really.
And that haughty tone of yours? It's silly
And unnecessary, for I would
Come and come again, for your own good.

CÉLIMÈNE: I'm sure that's true—if only in your mind.
But here's a truth that you and I might find:
There may come a time when I'll be you,
And be a prude and prim and I may rue
The days or months or years I lived this life
Of "jadery," as you would call it, rife
With joy and juices, filled with love songs sung

Under my window. But not now—I'm young.
And you can't tell me—if we're talking truth—
Real truth—does any human really "rue" their youth?
Unless they didn't grasp that horn of plenty
When they had the chance. Thank God I'm twenty!

ARSINOÉ: The issue of your age compared to mine,
Is such a minor point. One thinks of wine
And how it ages—

CÉLIMÈNE: —corked up, in the dark.

ARSINOÉ: What did you say? Ah, such a small remark
Could truly sabotage your reputation,
And suitors would depart in mass migration.
So, to this minor difference in our ages—
Trivial! To think it fires your rages!

CÉLIMÈNE: "My rages?" Wait. Oh, I see what you do—
You shift the subject and the point of view
So we are seeing my life only, where,
If we looked at yours, what would be there?
Admirers? Suitors? Any males at all?
Do only little dogs come when you call?
Tell you what, ma'am, if you think you can—
Take all my suitors, down to the last man!

ARSINOÉ: "All your suitors"—do you think I care?
And this huge number visiting your lair—
Who could not imagine the transaction
That must take place to merit all the action
These walls must see. For me, I think it's sad
That virtue, chastity, restraint are clad
In tattered, honest clothing, like a beggar
At the door of love, where there are
Never open hands to give the earthly
Gift of male attention to the worthy.
Because of this, I only can conclude
The way to get most men is to be lewd.

CÉLIMÈNE: Then do it. Be lewd. I applaud your spunk!
Go forth and live it—try it on a monk!
A priest, a bishop, stray men on the street!

ARSINOÉ: Oh, what a clever girl! Oh, aren't you sweet!
That's not my point, that's not what I am saying.
I say that's what you do, and I am praying
That you begin to live your life for virtue
Before your actions irrevocably hurt you.
Now, before we have a little spat,
I'll go. I would have gone before, but that
My carriage has not yet arrived.

CÉLIMÈNE: That's fine.
Do stay. I'd ask you if you want to dine,
But we're past that, surely you agree.
Here is the one you really came to see.

(ALCESTE *enters*)

ALCESTE: Célimèe!

CÉLIMÈNE: I see you have arrived.
And your arrest you seem to have survived.
Alceste, I have a note to write today,
That cannot be put off in any way.
Stay with Madam. I know she'll adjust.
I hate to be uncivil, yet I must.

(CÉLIMÈNE *exits.*)

Scene Five

(ALCESTE, ARSINOÉ)

ARSINOÉ: And so, she wants me to amuse you now.
You see, my carriage is detained somehow.
Nothing that I could think of would ensue
More charming than a tete-a-tete with you.
Men of outstanding worth inspire esteem,

And it's granted fairly, so it would seem.
Your effect on me is quite mysterious,
So much so that I become quite furious
When every day I see your worth neglected
And at court the honors misdirected.
I ask myself, "how can this be true?"
Yet every day nothing is done for you.

ALCESTE: Me? On what basis would my claim be
    tendered:
Great service to the state that I have rendered?
What could I have done so diligently,
That I'd complain that nothing's done for me?

ARSINOÉ: Those on whom is cast the eye of favor,
Are not the ones who merit what they savor.
Chance is their patron, as often as not,
While your merit—

ALCESTE: Talk like this is pure rot.
What king on earth would root out like some ferret,
And then reward each single person's merit?
My god, my merit's not worth this dissention.
Nothing in it "merits" this attention.

ARSINOÈ: Yet, singular merit certainly appeals
To those who see what character reveals.
You were praised in private, as of late,
By certain people of substantial weight.

ALCESTE: Since everyone is praised today, you see,
There's no great honor in it, especially.
Ech! We wade through it, right up to our ears,
In homage, tribute, praise—that's all one hears.
Our age insists it will equally bestow
Awards on every person we might know.
To illustrate how drastic it can get,
My valet has been praised in the Gazette!

ARSINOÉ: If you liked some position near the throne,
So to the court you could be better known.

One that you could warm to? With your say,
I could grease some wheels to smooth your way.

ALCESTE: What would you have me do there, then,
   Madam?
More a candidate for banishment, I am.
I wasn't born to breathe the air at court,
I don't have the muscles for the sport,
I don't have the language for deception,
I can't stand a half an hour reception!
Frankly, being frank is my great gift,
Yet every time I use it, there's a rift.
If I left court life I'd shut the door
On influence, prestige, privilege ever more.
But I would have my self-respect and ease,
Because I'd never have to lie to please.
The thousand cruel rebuffs that I've received,
The legal attacks under which I've grieved,
The simple-minded wits that I've endured,
The verse that grinds me down with every word:
To every one of these, I'd say good-bye,
To live a life of truth and never lie.

ARSINOÈ: Then I will forswear lying, sir, as well,
And bare my heart to you, and, frankly, tell
The truth of what I think about a subject.
It's intimate. I hope you won't object.
I would wish your ardor better placed,
And with a like proclivity embraced.
But, alas, my wish will not come true:
The one you love is not worthy of you.

ALCESTE: Now, Madam, I beg you to keep in mind,
This lady is your friend and has been kind.

ARSINOÉ: I know. But I, too, have my self-respect,
And I, too, have a truth I won't neglect.
I cannot stand to watch it, I'm afraid;
I have to tell you now, you are betrayed.

ALCESTE: How sweet of you to share with me this news.
Your purpose? To torment or just amuse?

ARSINOÉ: Since she is my friend, in her defense:
Inside her heart is only love's pretense.

ALCESTE: That may be; one can't see into hearts,
But one can always choose what one imparts.
I would have hoped your sense of charity
Might have held you back from telling me.

ARSINOÉ: I will say no more, if you prefer.
And we will never speak again of her.

ALCESTE: But, you see, you've put doubt in my mind,
And now it's like a spring that must unwind.
I only want to know, if we commence,
Those things for which there is clear evidence.

ARSINOÉ: Enough said. Your eyes will be the jury,
I won't add a word—you needn't worry.
Just see me home, and I will show you proof
Of her unfaithfulness and why she's been aloof.
And afterwards, if I may cajole you,
One might offer something to console you.

END OF ACT THREE

ACT FOUR

Scene One

(ÉLIANTE, PHILINTE)

PHILINTE: A more unyielding man has not been seen.
I thought some god would have to intervene.
Everyone tried everything to move him.
Even I tried gently to reprove him,
Suggesting that his stubbornness was foolish,
Obstinate, inflexible and mulish.
This did not go well. Of course, it wouldn't.
I tried to take it back and found I couldn't.
The lawyers were confused. I didn't blame them:
What were the objections, could we name them?
Officials wandered in from near and far,
They'd never seen a quarrel so bizarre.
"No, gentlemen," he said. "I'll not recant."
He turned to me: "It's heresy, Philinte.
To say a thing is good when it is not.
So I won't budge from this, no matter what."
And then, about Oronte, making it worse,
"Why does this man need me to like his verse?
Is his reputation somehow marred?
Will the world hold him in low regard?
In battle, would he be less of a fighter?
All because I say he's a bad writer?"
Ensuing silence yielded compromise:
"I'll praise his way of life, his style, his size,
His seat upon a horse, his swordsmanship,

The way he brings a cup up to his lip,
His dancing, the beauty of his home,
But I simply cannot, will not like his poem.
Furthermore," of course, he would proceed,
"Unless one writes it well, quite well, indeed,
One should swear off verse, leave rhyme alone.
Earn "I chose not to write," for one's headstone."
Finally, Alceste did have the wit
To soften his remarks, if just a bit:
"For being difficult, I apologize.
And so to the occasion I shall rise,
And tender my respect down to the letter,
And wish I would have liked your sonnet better."
Then those present made the two embrace,
So Oronte could exit with some grace.

ÉLIANTE: An unusual man is what I see,
Despite all his intractibility.
Truth at all costs, which some see as outrageous,
I find most heroic and courageous.
Though obstinance, I know, makes some dislike him,
I do wish there were more people like him.

PHILINTE: Could you be the one to share my wonder
At the awesome spell that he is under?
I'm speaking of his love for Célimène,
Who's doted on by half a dozen men,
Whose character could not be more different,
Who doesn't share, at all, his temperament.
For a man whose pride is overbearing,
To be in love at all is very daring.

ÉLIANTE: Thus is revealed love's complex mystery
With its disregard for compatibility.
Anyone in love knows mutual attraction
Has no rhyme or reason in its action.

PHILINTE: But do you think she loves him? Can you tell?

ÉLIANTE: She's young. She doesn't know herself that
  well.
Sometimes she's in love and doesn't know it.
Other times, she knows but doesn't show it.
And she also wont, as young girls are,
To fall for love itself, that distant star.

PHILINTE: With your cousin Célimène, Alceste
Will suffer love's abuses at their best.
If he felt as I do, his affection
Would have turned his head in your direction,
To the better choice, by far, in my mind.
He'd also know love is returned in kind.

ÉLIANTE: But how can I oppose his love of her?
With his best vision of her I concur.
She's my cousin. I find her very dear.
And this love of his seems quite sincere.
So I would genuinely rejoice
To see him with the lady of his choice.
However, in love's battle, if he loses,
Because another is the one she chooses,
Then I am here and willing to believe
Whatever love he brings I can receive.
Whatever words of love he's used to woo
First with someone else, I'll hear anew.

PHILINTE: With him, you know, I often plead your case,
Point to your character, beauty and grace.
So love of him I do not oppose.
However, this confession I'll disclose.
If it happens that these two are wed,
Would you consider loving me instead?

ÉLIANTE: You're just saying that, Philinte. Don't start.

PHILINTE: I'm speaking from the bottom of my heart.

Scene Two

(ALCESTE, ÉLIANTE, PHILINTE)

ALCESTE: Éliante, if you care anything for me,
You'll avenge this horrid infamy.

ÉLIANTE: What is it? What has upset you so?

ALCESTE: Something terrible I wish I didn't know!
A horrible disaster has brought me to my knees.
I'm overwhelmed. I'm speechless. Help me, please.

ÉLIANTE: Try to pull yourself together—

ALCESTE: And why?
Life has no meaning. Now I want to die!
Bewitching charm and such a beautiful face
On someone who's so odious and base—

ÉLIANTE: Who are you accusing?

ALCESTE: All is lost!
No love on earth is worth what this has cost!
I'm murdered! I'm betrayed! Assassinated!
All that I believed is violated!
Célimène...can't say it...misery.
Célimène has been unfaithful to me.

ÉLIANTE: Are you certain? What makes you think that's
   true?

PHILINTE: You know how jealousy can warp your view,
And make you see something that's just not there.

ALCESTE: Take your equivocations, go elsewhere!
I've had it with your stupid voice of reason!
(To ÉLIANTE)
Nothing could be truer than her treason.
In this pocket, I have such a letter.
As proof of love, it could not be better.

But it's a kind of proof I did not want,
A letter of such love, but to Oronte!
And written in her hand, those little curves.
So now we see what trusting someone serves.
I can't believe it! The disgrace and shame!
It's Oronte! I can barely speak his name.
The one I didn't fear! I was so sure
He didn't hold the least appeal for her.

PHILINTE: A letter may look much worse than it is.
We don't know why it's written, if it's his.

ALCESTE: Are you still here? I ask you, please, just go!

ÉLIANTE: This anger of yours doesn't help, you know.

ALCESTE: The only help for me must come from you.
Take my broken heart and make it new,
Free me from this overwhelming grief.
I turn to you for comfort and relief.
Avenge me on your cousin, then I'll rest.
Avenge me of this crime you must detest.

ÉLIANTE: Me? Avenge you? How?

ALCESTE: Accept my love.
You're the one I've thought so highly of.
We'll banish faithlessness by being true.
And I will punish her by loving you.
Each promise from my mouth into your ear,
Will punish her, because it is sincere.
Take me now. Let's not be circumspect.
I'll give you love, devotion, and respect.

ÉLIANTE: You're suffering. I know the pain you feel,
And what you offer me you think is real.
Rest easy. What you've offered isn't spurned,
But it is there because events have turned.
And they could turn again, and quickly, too,
How differently you'd feel, then, wouldn't you?
What if this sin is not quite what you fear?

Your need for vengeance will just disappear.
Yes, when we see a lover's innocence,
Our vengeful thoughts turn to benevolence.
For second choices, that's the end of that.
And The Great Schism? Just a lover's spat.

ALCESTE: No, no, I swear! She's hurt me mortally!
I won't go back. This is the end for me.
If ever I thought well of her again.
My soul would be imperiled by the sin.
She approaches. My rage I can't suppress!
I shall condemn her for her wickedness,
Unmask her fully, then, put at your feet
A heart that's cleansed of her artful deceit.

Scene Three

(CÉLIMÈNE, ALCESTE)

ALCESTE: Let me be the master of my feelings!

CÉLIMÈNE: You look upset. Is it your legal dealings?
If not, what is the matter with you now?
These constant angry looks will mark your brow.

ALCESTE: Of all the horrors humans can do, none—
Compares in any way to what you've done.
Mortal sins: sloth, rage and lechery
Look innocent next to your treachery.

CÉLIMÈNE: More sweet nothings? You'll make me shed
    a tear.

ALCESTE: Don't make a joke. There's nothing funny here.
You should be blushing. Lord, you have a reason:
I have solid proof of complete treason!
My heart, my eyes, and my divining star,
Warned "be vigilant, watch her near and far."
Yes, those suspicions you found so annoying,
Which you denied in words so sweet and cloying,

Were right, by god, and I was right to doubt.
And, oh, the crimes that I was right about!
I know that look, you think, "Oh, let him rant,
Soon he'll see things with a different slant."
No, I'll have revenge for this heartbreak:
I'll give to someone else those things you take,
And get them back! It's so hard to discover
One's worst thoughts are right about one's lover!
I know we have no power in desire,
And love ignites within us, like a fire,
Set by some cruel conqueror's torch
That every corner of our life will scorch.
But I would have no reason for complaint,
If you had just been honest, showed restraint,
Rejected my advances—one or two!
I would have found a way to forgive you.
But you dissembled and I felt embraced.
You covered up a truth I now have faced—
That you are evil, and what you did, pernicious.
No punishment you get could be as vicious.
My rage returns! It's clouding up my eyes!
And what is worse? Betrayal or your lies?
My reason's gone! I don't know what I'll do!
I feel like screaming when I'm close to you!

CÉLIMÈNE: You *are* screaming. At least, it seems to me.
What is the reason for this insanity?

ALCESTE: Yes, I am insane! I've lost my mind!
I took poison from one I thought was kind.
As a witch's brew it was decanted;
I was murdered as I was enchanted.

CÉLIMÈNE: What betrayal are you complaining of?

ALCESTE: Such duplicity! Such betrayal of love!
Watch the betrayer get what she deserves!
It's your handwriting. See your little curves?
Look how this evil note is executed,
And then tell me this proof can be refuted.

CÉLIMÈNE: This is why you had this awful fit?

ALCESTE: You're not blushing looking at it?

CÉLIMÈNE: Why would I blush looking at this note?

ALCESTE: Because it's clearly something that you wrote.
All right, no signature, but see the hand?

CÉLIMÈNE: Of course, I see it. I wrote the note. And?

ALCESTE: You can stand there, caught, no trace of
    shame,
For crimes against my passion and my name?

CÉLIMÈNE: You are, in truth, the most ridiculous man.

ALCESTE: Oh yes, try to deny it, if you can!
Insult and slander me, as is your wont,
But don't deny this missive to Oronte.

CÉLIMÈNE: Oronte! A note to him? Who told you that?

ALCESTE: The one who gave it to me? But so what?
If you had written it to anyone,
It's just as damning. Look how you've begun!
These endearments, how do you explain?

CÉLIMÈNE: I wrote it to a woman—it's so plain.
Are you still insulted? Are you still raging?

ALCESTE: Ah! Good diversion in this war we're waging.
There's an answer I did not expect,
I don't deny this moment of respect.
And here I am, convinced and nearly silent.
But wait a minute! Now I'm feeling violent!
How dare you perpetrate this shabby ruse?
Is there no deception you won't use?
These words of passion are meant for a friend?
Let me read some lines—

CÉLIMÈNE: Let's call an end
To this. The conversation's through.
You treat me like a subject. You—

You have no authority over me.
And all the things you've said? Malignancy!

ALCESTE: No, no, no cause to get upset, just read,
And clear yourself and satisfy my need.

CÉLIMÈNE: Oh, I can't get upset, but you can rage.
And all because of letters on a page.

ALCESTE: Please. I'll be happy, if I can know
It's for a woman. Please, just make it so.

CÉLIMÈNE: It's for Oronte. That's what you should see:
Me, receiving him, at nights, lovingly.
Admiring what he says, with passion brimming.
There. Your scene's complete. My head is swimming.

ALCESTE: Could anything more cruel be contrived?
My heart just died, I'll have to be revived.
I face her with a list of crimes this long,
She turns around and I'm the one who's wrong.
My suspicions pushed to the very limit,
But, oh, this light of love, if I could dim it!
It burns into my soul, like a hot ember.
Had I a life before? I don't remember.
She glories in my misery and my pain.
I'm bound to her by some unbreakable chain!
(To CÉLIMÈNE)
Traitoress! You know this perfectly well.
You see my weakness to put me in Hell.
My love for you is fatal and you use it.
I've so much love, you know you can abuse it,
And you do. Now be kind and please repent.
Stop pretending to be guilty! Be innocent!
Take this letter, prove to me it's true,
It's written to a woman and from you.
Take it! And then we'll finally leave it.
Whatever you say, I'll make myself believe it.

CÉLIMÈNE: When you're this jealous, I can't talk to you.
You don't deserve my love. That's what is true.

Go! No, wait. I'd like you to tell me,
What you think could possibly compel me
To descend to these depths of deception
That you think you've traced to their inception?
If, truly, my heart leaned another way,
Why would I hide it? Why wouldn't I just say,
"I love another." No, I've said clearly,
"You're the one I love." I spoke sincerely.
In women, there's a natural reticence
To candidly admit our sentiments.
An "honorable woman" does not reveal
Whom she really loves. She must conceal
Her feelings for the one she loves, and so
Her passion's always secret, none can know.
Men declare their love to win a heart.
When women do the same, lovers depart.
In spite of this, you had my admission.
Yet your reply to me was gross suspicion.
You're the angry one? Well, I'm angry, too.
I wonder why I ever cared for you.
I'm an idiot. I'm an imbecile.
I have shown a decided lack of will.
I'll take a public lover and be zealous,
And give you a good reason to be jealous.

ALCESTE: Is this the truth you're telling me right now?
How can I believe it? Tell me how.
You see, my weakness for you makes me wonder:
Can I trust her? Is it some spell I'm under?
It doesn't matter—it's my destiny.
To hope. And see how it enslaves me?
Yet I stay and, no doubt, will discover
You're vile enough to have another lover.

CÉLIMÈNE: Love, for you, is only in possession.
You don't know how to love—it's just obsession.
You don't really love me, not a bit.

ALCESTE: My love for you is boundless, infinite.
My love for you is more than I can name.
Would you believe me if I did proclaim
To all the living world, both near and far?
I wish you could be other than you are:
Reduced to misery, unloved and poor,
With no status, creditors at your door,
No family or friends to comfort you,
No property, nothing to see you through.
Then I could really love you as one ought,
Repairing each injustice fate has brought,
Lift you up and have this joy and glory:
My enormous love has changed your story.

CÉLIMÈNE: I'd rather that you simply wished me well.
May heaven save me from this tale you tell!
What now? your valet!

Scene Four

(DU BOIS, CÉLIMÈNE, ALCESTE)

ALCESTE: Why is he disguised?
Some prank?

DU BOIS: Sir...

ALCESTE: Well?

DU BOIS: I can't be recognized.

ALCESTE: Why not?

DU BOIS: The situation's getting thick.

ALCESTE: Speak.

DU BOIS: Shall I speak aloud?

ALCESTE: And make it quick.

DU BOIS: Are we enough alone?

ALCESTE: Of course we are.
What's going on?

DU BOIS: Sir, you may go very far.

ALCESTE: What do you mean?

DU BOIS: Sir, it's a necessity.

ALCESTE: What?

DU BOIS: A journey's in your future. Come with me.

ALCESTE: Why?

DU BOIS: You need to leave and quickly, too.

ALCESTE: Because?

DU BOIS: You have to. No good-byes for you.

ALCESTE: You're my valet. Tell me. I'm in trouble?

DU BOIS: You could say that. Clear out on the double.

ALCESTE: Du Bois, calm down. I want you to explain.
But no more riddles, in language clear and plain.

DU BOIS: A man in a black coat and angry face,
Came to your house and left a note—someplace,
In the kitchen, yes—scribbled, hard to read,
Scary enough to put me off my feed.
Something to do with your trial, no doubt,
But even Satan couldn't make it out.

ALCESTE: That's all? A person leaves a note and goes.
And this is how this need for flight arose?

DU BOIS: That is what I'm telling you. There's more.
Another man came later to the door,
And, in a hurry, asked if you were there.
You weren't. And since I tend to your welfare,
And am so able, it's garnered me some fame,
He gave me the task of...what is his name?

ALCESTE: Forget the name. What did he say to you?

DU BOIS: It's one of your friends. That'll have to do.
He told me you must flee. I did my best.
And that you are threatened with arrest.

ALCESTE: Arrest? But why? Was he more specific?

DU BOIS: He wrote you a note. His style's terrific.
Something about a book. It's mysterious.
Did you slander someone? Sure sounds serious.

ALCESTE: Give me the note.

CÉLIMÈNE: What is this about?

ALCESTE: I'm sure I don't know, but I will find out.
Why can't you just find it? You're not able?

DU BOIS: I guess I must have left it on the table.

ALCESTE: You are a dead man!

CÉLIMÈNE: Why don't you just go,
And fix this "peril". I'm afraid to know.

ALCESTE: However hard I try, it seems that fate,
Has totally refused to allocate
A single discrete moment in this day
For us to speak and finish what we say.
To triumph over fate, Madam, permit me
To come back later, if you will admit me.

END OF ACT FOUR

ACT FIVE

Scene One

(ALCESTE, PHILINTE)

ALCESTE: I am resolved. My mind's made up. That's it.

PHILINTE: Of all the blows, why this one? Why permit...

ALCESTE: Argue all you want, but you will find,
Nothing you can say will change my mind.
Yes, I've been dealing with adversity,
But this last blow is pure perversity.
I'm retiring from the human race.
There's not one whit of honor in this place.
I believed in truth, justice, principle;
With these, I should have been invincible.
The rightness of my cause was known to all,
Yet from that honored height they let me fall.
No, I was pushed and we both know by whom,
That evil scoundrel from the depths of doom.
This simple, awful fact I have to face,
Though right was on my side, I lost my case!
If that's not enough evil for a day,
He has the pure audacity to say,
That I'm the author of some horrid book,
That obviously was written by some crook
To capitalize on people's worst desires.
And then, you know who's fanning all the fires?
Oronte! Of course! He's murmuring in each ear,
Making sure my authorship is clear.

This awful book that I think should be banned,
The world sees as a product of my hand.
Because our friend Oronte is being spiteful.
Can you deny my comments were insightful?
He came to me with verses that were bad.
He asked me what I thought. I made him mad.
You were there. You saw that he insisted.
To tell him what I thought, I first resisted,
And tried to put him off because I knew
Those who want the truth are very few.
He has respect at court and he's my enemy!
And in his heart he'll never pardon me.
And why? For perpetrating some falsehood?
No. I didn't find his sonnet to be good.
And so, dear God above, behold mankind!
Show me, where's that shred of good you find?
For me, I won't wait for one more mishap,
Let's leave this trackless forest, this death-trap,
Where human wolves all decency subdue.
Deceivers! I refuse to live with you!

PHILINTE: Could you think a bit before you go?
Things are not as bad as that, you know.
What you're charged with, whatever it may be,
Can't have that much credence—you're still free.
It's bad to file complaints that are not true.
It may hurt your opponent more than you.

ALCESTE: Him? What hurt he gets will be minimal.
He has free license to be criminal.
His reputation? It will surely grow,
Now he's someone everyone will know.

PHILINTE: Oh, I don't think he's getting real attention.
Of his attack on you, there's been no mention.
The rumor of this book? I think that's moot.
And I think you should appeal your lawsuit,
With whatever judgment—

ALCESTE: I'll accept it.
On the books, as is, I'll let it sit.
I wouldn't think of having it erased:
Such evidence of rightness so debased.
I want it recorded for posterity,
To show the future the pathetic rarity
Of any signs of justice in this age.
They'll have the proof, at least, and they can gauge
How abundant is the testimony
Of our wicked times, vicious and phony.
I'll lose the money. Whatever it may cost:
Twenty thousand francs are francs well lost.
For twenty thousand francs, I get to curse
All of humankind as it gets worse.

PHILINTE: But after all, my friend—

ALCESTE: Yes, after all,
When will your excuses hit the wall?
Look at me, Sir. What can you say to me.
Will nothing shake your equanimity?

PHILINTE: I agree with everything you say,
Fraud, deceit, self-interest rules the day.
Cabals and cliques conspire, near and far.
And all men should be different than they are.
This sense of natural justice that they lack,
Is that a reason to go home and pack?
These human defects we can't help but see,
Aren't they the reason for philosophy?
What insights would we have that we could trust,
If nothing countered what we know is just?
And if all hearts were frank, true and obedient,
Virtue would be common, thus, expedient.
And learning tolerance and endurance—

ALCESTE: Sir, do let me give you this assurance,
Your reasoning is matched by eloquence,
But how can I, in truth, let you commence,
When you're wasting all that wise propriety,

On someone who's retiring from society?
My reasoning—I have some—says don't stay here.
I can't control my tongue, that much is clear.
I can't control what I may say tomorrow,
It seems my views will always bring me sorrow.
I'll wait for Célimène. Don't argue—leave.
She must agree with what I now believe.
If she loves me, really, we will see.
This is her last chance to prove it to me.

PHILINTE: Let's wait for her and sit with Éliante.

ALCESTE: No, I'm much too troubled. No, I can't.
You go there and leave me here to brood.
I'll sit in this dark corner with my mood.

PHILINTE: Well, that's bad company. Stay here until
I get Éliante to join us, if she will.

Scene Two

(ORONTE, CÉLIMÈNE, ALCESTE)

ORONTE: Yes, if you want to, you only need say,
And we will tie the knots of love today.
But I need some assurance that you love me,
And do not put someone else above me.
So, dear lady, please don't hesitate,
An ardent lover cannot stand to wait.
If my passion has had its affect,
I ask you for this proof of your respect:
All your ties with Alceste you must sever,
And from your house and life, ban him forever.

CÉLIMÈNE: What has happened to your admiration,
To turn it into such a condemnation?

ORONTE: That troubled topic needs no clarity.
I want to know how you feel about me.

I need to know if I will win or lose,
The moment's come, my dear, for you to choose.

ALCESTE: (*Appearing from the dark corner where he has been
lurking*) Yes, the gentleman is right. It's up to you.
His request has voiced what I want, too.
The same ardor drives me, the same concern.
Whom will you accept, whom will you spurn?
I, too, want to hear which one's your choice,
No more waiting. It's time to give it voice.

ORONTE: I don't want, in my untimely passion,
To thwart your fortune, sir, in any fashion.

ALCESTE: And I don't want, in my state of jealousy,
To share her, sir. I mean that zealously.

ORONTE: If you're the one who truly has her heart—

ALCESTE: If she loves you with even one small part—

ORONTE: I swear to you to make no further claim.

ALCESTE: I swear to you to forget her name.

ORONTE: Madam, you may speak without constraint.

ALCESTE: Whatever you decide, there's no complaint.

ORONTE: Our hearts are yours. We leave it up to you.

ALCESTE: You only have to choose between us two.

ORONTE: You refuse to speak? Why are you staring?

ALCESTE: Why do you hesitate? Are you comparing?

CÉLIMÈNE: Who do you think you are? And who am I?
Some servant choosing loins of beef to buy?
Of course I know which one of you I favor.
You think you see me hesitate and waver,
When nothing could be easier than to choose,
My choice was made before. But I refuse
To publicly declare who is preferred.
In private should such tiding, then, be heard.

Asking me to blurt out how I feel
In front of both of you, makes my head reel!
Is it wrong that a heart should be inclined
To be partial without being so unkind
As, in his rival's presence, tell a man
He hasn't won your love and never can.

ORONTE: Let me have the truth and I'll withstand it.
I just want honesty.

ALCESTE: And I demand it.
Let the truth burst on the scene and speak!
Spare me nothing. Do you think I'm weak?
I see, to keep your lovers, you've been clever,
Pleasing everyone is your endeavor.
Well, you can't do that now. We won't let you.
Be blunt and let one of us forget you.
And if you're silent, even that won't do,
I'll assume that's a rejection from you.

ORONTE: I'm indebted, Sir, for this outburst!
I only wish that I had said it first!

CÉLIMÈNE: A tantrum in tandem! Something to see!
You love justice? Where is it for me?
You can yell and scream into the night,
I won't do something I don't think is right.
Here's Éliante. Let's ask her to judge.

Scene Three

(ÉLIANTE, PHILINTE, CÉLIMÈNE, ORONTE, ALCESTE)

CÉLIMÈNE: Though I'm persecuted, I won't budge.
These gentlemen, once enemies, now allies,
Demand that I do something I despise,
And that would be to publicly impart
The final, private preference of my heart.
This would, of course, immediately banish

One of them, who, then, expects to vanish.
Éliante, you tell them. It's not done!

ÉLIANTE: Do not ask me that. I'm the wrong someone.
You won't like what you hear because you'll find
I prefer that someone speaks her mind.

ORONTE: It seems that you defend yourself in vain.

ALCESTE: It seems that your evasions meet disdain.

ORONTE: You must, you must speak out and make your
choice.

ALCESTE: Or it will speak in the absence of your voice.

ORONTE: You can end this torment with a sound.

ALCESTE: I hear you now. Your silence is profound.

Scene Four

(ACASTE, CLITANDRE, ARSINOÉ, PHILINTE, ÉLIANTE,
ORONTE, CÉLIMÈNE, ALCESTE)

ACASTE: *(To* CÉLIMÈNE*)*
We have come in one shared occupation
And that's to clarify a situation.

CLITANDRE: *(To* ORONTE *and* ALCESTE*)*
To find you here, how very à propos,
For both of you are part of this, you know.

ARSINOÉ: Madam, you must be surprised to see me,
But I am here on a mission of mercy.
These gentlemen came to me as a friend,
With an offense I could not comprehend.
I respect you too much at this time,
To think you capable of such a crime.
In the face of such strong evidence,
I never lost an ounce of confidence.
Our friendship's stronger than our differences,

And stronger than these proofs and inferences.
So I am here, not to reprimand her,
But to watch her clear herself of slander.

ACASTE: The penmanship of this could well indict it.
This letter to Clitandre. Did you write it?
One wonders when your decency was lost.

CLITANDRE: Long before you wrote this to Acaste.

ACASTE: *(To* ORONTE *and* ALCESTE*)*
The handwriting, I believe, you'll recognize;
The lady is more garrulous than wise.
The little curves of pen we all should heed.
But listen as I give this one a read:

"My Dear Strange Clitandre: To condemn me for being
cheerful and then to reproach me by claiming that I'm
never so joyous as when I am not with you, is unjust
and strange. And, if you don't come right away to beg
my forgiveness for this offense, I will never forgive you.
In my whole life. About our great beanpole of a
viscount—"

Pity he's not here.

"Our great beanpole of a viscount, whom you put at the
top of your ridiculous list of people you think delight
me more than I'm delighted by you: I am not eager to
see that odd-looking man again. Since the day I saw
him stand for three quarters of an hour, spitting into a
well to watch the circles form, I have had a rather low
opinion of him. As for the little marquess—"

That would be me, Acaste, everyone—not to be vain
about it.

"As for the little marquess, who sat holding my hand
for hours yesterday, he is such a total nonentity. And
he's dirt poor, owns nothing but his sword, the only
remnant of his once-noble family. The sword is not in

good condition. As for the man with the green ribbons
that he insists on wearing—"

(To ALCESTE) Your turn, sir. Isn't this fun?

"As for the man with the green ribbons that he insists
on wearing—he amuses me sometimes with his
bluntness and his bursts of anger; but most of the time
he's the most annoying man in the world. As for the
sonneteer—"

(To ORONTE) I'm afraid that's you, sir.

"As for the sonneteer. He insists he's a wit and will be a
writer in spite of everyone. I can't make myself listen to
what he has to say—his prose is as boring as his verse.
So, my dear strange Clitandre, do you finally believe
that I am not as wonderfully entertained as you think?
That I miss you more than I can say at all those dreary
parties I am dragged to? And that the presence of
people one loves is the best seasoning to any pleasures
one enjoys."

CLITANDRE: Now it's my turn. And soon we will see,
What our Letter Writer says about me.

"My dear Acaste, You mention Clitandre—"

And that would be me, her dear strange one.

"Clitandre who constantly plays the languishing lover,
however, he is the last man on earth I'd ever love.
He's insane to believe that I'm in love with him,
just as you are insane to believe that I don't love you.
So see things from his point of view, believe I love you.
Then, do come to see me as often as you can to help me
bear the misery of his obsession with me."

More portraits, this time written with a pen:
"A Portrait of Your Friends" by Célimène.
That's enough. These Former Friends depart
To show the town this portrait of your heart.

ACASTE: I could say something in repudiation,
But you're not worthy of my indignation.
There are women with a secure largesse,
Eager to console this 'little marquess.'

ORONTE: How could you ridicule me so completely?
You've written me so many notes so sweetly.
I see you now, behind that lovely face,
Promising love to the whole human race!
I was your dupe. I won't be any longer.
That which does not break me makes me stronger.
You've done me a favor. I'm strangely free.
I think that you've returned my heart to me.
Yes. It's back. And in true health, endures.
And my revenge is that the loss is yours.
(To ALCESTE*)*
I leave the field to you, needless to say,
With this lady, you can come to terms today.

ARSINOÉ: *(To* CÉLIMÈNE*)*
Well. I, for one, simply can't allow
My silence to continue. No, not now.
This has got to be the most malicious;
The level of atrocity is vicious.
Toward others, I could care less how you act,
But him, you've had the fortune to attract,
Yes, him, who worships you, this worthy man,
How could—

ALCESTE: Madam, allow me, if you can,
To handle my own interests in this matter.
To help or not help me: choose the latter.
In future, anything to do with me,
I want you to avoid entirely.
And the guarding of my heart? I want recorded,
Your great zeal will never be rewarded.
If my love I avenged, with someone new,
The choice would never, ever fall on you.

ARSINOÉ: Hah! I had hopes, sir? That's what you
   believed?
Well, from that fabrication be relieved.
And let me disabuse you of those lies;
You are hardly what I'd call a prize.
Before you go: I pray you stay attached,
To this jade, with whom you're aptly matched.
My kind of people aren't for such as you,
I'd aim less high. In fact, you have. Adieu.
(*She exits.*)

ALCESTE: Through all of this, I've been very quiet,
Exercised control, you can't deny it.
May I now—

CÉLIMÈNE: Say whatever you need to.
Followed by what censure it may lead to.
You have every right and should complain;
Whatever my excuses, they're in vain.
Of all of them, I treated you the fairest,
But it was wrong, and, frankly, I'm embarrassed.
For the anger of the others, I have no time.
But against you, I admit my crime.
I know you must resent me and that's fair,
I know that it must seem that I don't care,
Your anger's just, please, go ahead, berate me,
You have every reason now to hate me.
Do so, I consent to it.

ALCESTE: With this admission,
I'm to hate you and with your permission?
As if I'd triumph over my infatuation?
I'd love to hate you, end all the frustration.
But will my heart obey me? I don't think so.
(*To* ÉLIANTE *and* PHILINTE)
I'm afraid there's more, so please don't go.
You will be the witnesses to my defect,
And see what shameless passion can effect.
To show how wrong it is to call men wise,

I'm going to fall farther, before your eyes.
(*To* CÉLIMÈNE)
Your infamous behavior, I'll forget,
All your tricks and insults are no threat,
When I see them, simply, as your way
Of yielding to the vices of the day.
All that is the past, if you'll agree
To put your hand in mine and follow me,
To a distant, untamed, trackless place
Where, to look upon a human face
Is rare. Come now, because I've sworn to go,
Where solitude and you are all I'll know.
It's the way for you to make amends,
For the harm you did to all your friends.
There you can atone, and if you will,
I can permit myself to love you still.

CÉLIMÈNE: You want me to renounce the world and go
To lose myself some place I do not know?

ALCESTE: Yes, if you want my love and share my
    passion,
What's the world but so much empty fashion?
Aren't I enough for you? Aren't I plenty?

CÉLIMÈNE: That kind of life is frightening when you're
    twenty;
I don't have the strength and fortitude,
To join you in such total solitude.
Where my world would only be we two.
However, if my hand I offered you,
And you were satisfied with my true vow,
I would resolve—

ALCESTE: My heart detests you now.
Worse than anything you've said or done before,
This rejection cuts me to the core.
The verdict's as devastating as it's true:
You're everything to me—I'm not, to you.
I refuse you and, from this moment, sever

All ties to you and release myself forever.
(*To* ÉLIANTE)
You, Madame, are nothing but sincere,
And you deserve someone to hold you dear.
I know that in the past I may have hurt you,
But I esteem your beauty and your virtue.
Allow me to continue to admire you.
I have a troubled heart and can't aspire to
The honor of your hand. I realize,
I will never have those worthy ties.
I hope, therefore, you do not feel rejected—

ÉLIANTE: This is not the answer you expected.
My hand is unavailable, you see,
Because of this man standing near to me.
Your friend, Philinte, I think, would answer you,
He'd take my hand, if offered, and I do.

PHILINTE: Éliante, if you would be my wife,
It would be the honor of my life.

ALCESTE: May you, to have true happiness, avow
To hold on to these feelings you have now.
While I, destined to tell a tragic tale,
Leave this world of treachery and betrayal,
And search the earth for someplace I'll be free
To live my life with truth and honesty.

PHILINTE: Éliante, let's go, do anything we can,
To get him to give up this hopeless plan.

END OF PLAY

PLAYS BY NEAL BELL
MCTEAGUE: A TALE OF SAN FRANCISCO
RAGGED DICK
THÉRÈSE RAQUIN

PLAYS BY PHIL BOSAKOWSKI
BIERCE TAKES ON THE RAILROAD!
CHOPIN IN SPACE
NIXON APOLOGIZES TO THE NATION

PLAYS BY ALAN BOWNE
BEIRUT
FORTY-DEUCE
SHARON AND BILLY

PLAYS BY MICHAEL BRADY
KORCZAK'S CHILDREN
TO GILLIAN ON HER 37TH BIRTHDAY
TWO BEARS BLINKING

PLAYS BY LONNIE CARTER
LEMUEL
GULLIVER
GULLIVER REDUX

PLAYS BY STEVE CARTER
DAME LORRAINE
HOUSE OF SHADOWS
MIRAGE
ONE LAST LOOK
TEA ON INAUGURATION DAY

PLAYS BY ANTON CHEKHOV
ADAPTED BY RICHARD NELSON
THE SEAGULL
THREE SISTERS
THE WOOD DEMON

PLAYS BY ANTHONY CLARVOE
LET'S PLAY TWO
THE LIVING
SHOW AND TELL

PLAYS BY LAURA SHAINE CUNNINGHAM
BANG
BEAUTIFUL BODIES
CRUSING CLOSE TO CRAZY

PLAYS BY MICHAEL MCGUIRE
THESE FLOWERS ARE FOR MY MOTHER
HOLD ME
HELEN'S PLAY

PLAYS BY JANET NEIPRIS
A SMALL DELEGATION
ALMOST IN VEGAS
THE AGREEMENT

PLAYS BY RICHARD NELSON
EARLY PLAYS VOLUME ONE
CONJURING AN EVENT
JUNGLE COUP
THE KILLING OF YABLONSKI
SCOOPING

PLAYS BY RICHARD NELSON
EARLY PLAYS VOLUME TWO
BAL
THE RETURN OF PINOCCHIO
THE VIENNA NOTES

PLAYS BY RICHARD NELSON
EARLY PLAYS VOLUME THREE
AN AMERICAN COMEDY
JITTERBUGGING: SCENES OF SEX IN A NEW SOCIETY
RIP VAN WINKLE, OR "THE WORKS"

PLAYS BY EUGENE O'NEILL
EARLY FULL-LENGTH PLAYS
BEYOND THE HORIZON
THE EMPEROR JONES
ANNA CHRISTIE

PLAYS BY ERIC OVERMYER
DARK RAPTURE
IN PERPETUITY THROUGHOUT THE UNIVERSE
ON THE VERGE

PLAYS BY ROCHELLE OWENS
CHUCKY'S HUNCH
FUTZ
KONTRAPTION
THREE FRONT

ADAPTATIONS OF THE CLASSICS

ALKI (PEER GYNT)

AMPHITRYON

ANYTHING TO DECLARE?

THE BROTHERS KARAMAZOV

A CHRISTMAS CAROL

DEAD SOULS

DON JUAN

DON QUIXOTE DE LA JOLLA

THE FATHER

FIGARO/FIGARO

FRANK LANGELLA'S CYRANO

IL CAMPIELO

THE ILLUSION

JITTERBUGGING: SCENES OF SEX FROM A NEW SOCIETY
(LA RONDE)

THE MARRIAGE OF FIGARO

MCTEAGUE: A TALE OF SAN FRANCISCO

THE MISANTHROPE

MISS JULIE

MONSTER (FRANKENSTEIN)

PLAYBOY OF THE WEST INDIES

THE PROMISE (THE DYBBUK)

THE SEAGULL

THÉRÈSE RAQUIN

THREE SISTERS

THE WOOD DEMON